HEGEL'S DIALECTICAL LOGIC

HEGEL'S DIALECTICAL LOGIC

Ermanno Bencivenga

OXFORD
UNIVERSITY PRESS

2000

OXFORD

UNIVERSITY PRESS

Oxford   New York
Athens   Auckland   Bangkok   Bogotá   Buenos Aires   Calcutta
Cape Town   Chennai   Dar es Salaam   Delhi   Florence   Hong Kong   Istanbul
Karachi   Kuala Lumpur   Madrid   Melbourne   Mexico City   Mumbai
Nairobi   Paris   São Paulo   Shanghai   Singapore   Taipei   Tokyo   Toronto   Warsaw

and associated companies in
Berlin   Ibadan

Copyright © 2000 by Oxford University Press

Published by Oxford University Press, Inc.
198 Madison Avenue, New York, New York 10016

Oxford is a registered trademark of Oxford University Press.

Library of Congress Cataloging-in-Publication Data
Bencivenga, Ermanno, 1950–
Hegel's dialectical logic / by Ermanno Bencivenga.
p.   cm.
Includes bibliographical references and index.
ISBN 0-19-513829-5
1. Hegel, Georg Wilhelm Friedrich, 1770–1831—Contributions
in logic.   2. Logic, Modern.   I. Title.
B2949.L8 B46   2001
193—dc21   99-087455

1 3 5 7 9 8 6 4 2

Printed in the United States of America
on acid-free paper

PREFACE

My first two books dealt with free logics: formal systems which address and try to resolve the charge that the most basic contemporary canons of reasoning (those codified in "classical" quantification theory) are infected with existential assumptions. At the time, keeping logic independent of ontology seemed to me, on the face of it, a reasonable enough task. If requested for motivation, I would have proffered something like the following: "Suppose you want to prove the existence of God, or the nonexistence of the largest prime. Then you would not want that the very logical tools you use in your proof already automatically commit you to the existence of God, or indeed of the largest prime—and you would not want to be forced to awkward reformulations of your statements in order to avoid such commitments." That, for me in my twenties, was that.

Then came Kant. Or, I should say, came an understanding of him—because the man and his work had been in the background for quite a while. And, with my understanding of Kant, came the centrality of ethics: of philosophy as practical reason, as deontic to the core, as intrinsically normative. As that picture got entrenched, the task of disconnecting our ways of thinking from any involvement in actuality became increasingly urgent: it wasn't just a matter of allowing for more elegant and efficient proofs—my social role as an intellectual was at stake.

In an article published in the 1980s, "Free from What?", I argued for an intimate conceptual connection between free logics and Kant's transcendental idealism. But it was only at the beginning of the 1990s that I finally began to face the contamination of logic with ontology in its most monumental, and most dangerous, form: because only then did I turn my concentrated attention to Hegel. Once again, he had been sitting in the shade for a while; but it was only then that I was ready for him—only then did I see light shine on his texts. There began a very strange kind of involvement, in which awe was mixed with fright, and intellectual respect with moral rejection. And, eventually, this book came about: as the outcome of this peculiar encounter and as an (ironically) all-too-Hegelian vindication of those early logical steps of mine.

I thank Daniel Berthold-Bond, Bill Bristow, and three anonymous Oxford readers for their comments on earlier drafts of this work, and all of the many participants in my various Hegel courses, seminars, and workshops for their penetrating comments, suggestions, and criticisms.

Irvine, California   *E. B.*
March 2000

CONTENTS

NOTE ON TEXTS

All Aristotle references are to *The Complete Works of Aristotle,* edited by Jonathan Barnes (Princeton: Princeton University Press, 1984). For each reference I have provided the page number(s) and the specific treatise from which it comes. I have used the following abbreviations:

Cat.	*Categories*
De Int.	*De Interpretatione*
Eud. Eth.	*Eudemian Ethics*
Gen. of An.	*Generation of Animals*
Hist. of An.	*History of Animals*
Met.	*Metaphysics*
Meteor.	*Meteorology*
Nic. Eth.	*Nicomachean Ethics*
Parts	*Parts of Animals*
Post. An.	*Posterior Analytics*
Progr. of An.	*Progression of Animals*
Sense	*Sense and Sensibilia*
Soph. Ref.	*Sophistical Refutations*

Most Hegel references are to English translations of his works. Unless otherwise noted, I have made only the following slight revisions of these translations: I have deleted a number of capitalizations; I have constantly translated "der Begriff" as "the concept" and "der Geist" as "the spirit"; and I have uniformed spelling and typographical conventions (this last remark applies to the Aristotle quotes as well). Abbreviations and bibliographical details for the translations I have used are as follows:

Aesthetics   *Aesthetics: Lectures on Fine Art.* 2 vols. Translated by T. Knox. Oxford: Clarendon Press, 1975.

Difference   *The Difference between Fichte's and Schelling's System of Philosophy.* Edited by H. Harris and W. Cerf. Albany: SUNY Press, 1977.

Faith   *Faith and Knowledge.* Edited by W. Cerf and H. Harris. Albany: SUNY Press, 1977.

History   *The Philosophy of History.* Translated by J. Sibree. Buffalo: Prometheus Books, 1991.

Krug   "How the Ordinary Human Understanding Takes Philosophy (as Displayed in the Works of Mr. Krug)." Translated by H. Harris in *Between Kant and Hegel,* edited by G. di Giovanni and H. Harris. 292–310. Albany: SUNY Press, 1985.

Logic   *The Encyclopaedia Logic.* Translated by T. Geraets, W. Suchting, and H. Harris. Indianapolis: Hackett, 1991.

Mind   *Philosophy of Mind.* Translated by A. Miller. Oxford: Clarendon Press, 1971.

Nature   *Philosophy of Nature.* Translated by A. Miller. Oxford: Clarendon Press, 1970.

Phenomenology   *Phenomenology of Spirit.* Translated by A. Miller. Oxford: Oxford University Press, 1977.

Philosophy I, II, and III   *Lectures on the History of Philosophy.* 3 vols. Translated by E. Haldane. Lincoln: University of Nebraska Press, 1995.

Religion I, II, and III   *Lectures on the Philosophy of Religion.* 3 vols. Edited by P. Hodgson. Berkeley: University of California Press, 1984, 1987, and 1985.

Right   *Elements of the Philosophy of Right.* Edited by A. Wood. Cambridge: Cambridge University Press, 1991.

Science   *Science of Logic.* Translated by A. Miller. London: Allen and Unwin, 1969.

For Hegel's *On the Orbits of Planets* I have used the *Gesammelte Werke,* edited by M. Baum and K. Meist, vol. 5 (Hamburg: Meiner,

1998), 233–53. For the German originals of the above translations I have used the *Werke,* edited by E. Moldenhauer and K. Michel (Frankfurt: Suhrkamp, 1969–1971), and the *Vorlesungen über die Philosophie der Religion,* edited by W. Jaeschke (Hamburg: Meiner, 1983–1985).

For references other than those above, see the bibliography at the end of the book.

HEGEL'S DIALECTICAL LOGIC

INTRODUCTION

Several times over the last ten years, as I painstakingly worked my way through Hegel's corpus, I asked myself what kind of book (if any) I should write about him. The imposing majesty of his texts evoked longings for similarly comprehensive architectures; the startling vistas opened by many of his individual steps suggested careful, diligent unpacking, lest the jargon smother the precious intuitions deposited there; the complex, creative borrowings from other philosophers—or of other philosophers from him—as well as the deep, revealing antagonisms with yet others (or with the same ones) seemed to demand an elaborate, detailed taxonomy. Eventually, I decided to do none of the above; and here I want to explain why.

The fact that I am a logician by training may have something to do with it—but, whether or not it does, I convinced myself early that Hegel's most fundamental contribution is his logic, in three ways. First, his powerful and controversial views about art, religion, science, the state, and virtually every other major (and many a not-so-major) subject can only be the views they are because of how he reasons; people who reason differently could well commit themselves to saying that Christianity is the culmination of religion or that the state realizes concrete freedom—that is, to statements quite literally identical to some of Hegel's own—and yet have those statements mean something vastly different from what they mean for him.

Second, in contrast with its main competition—Aristotelian, analytic logic—Hegel's dialectical "tool" is much more than that. It is no organon to be prefixed to science proper, no neutral site where various "empirical" views may be indifferently entertained, no lofty distancing oneself in purified abstractions. Because of what tool it is, it will pervade and appropriate every subject matter, reveal it as conceptually structured through and through—indeed, as nothing other than conceptually structured. It will supersede the distinction between a concept and its instances, and make every particular existence, however modest, however local, a matter of logical concern. So it's not just (as per the previous paragraph) that analytic and dialectical logicians will mean something very different by the same statement about art; it is also that the latter will turn that statement into one belonging to the *logic* of art.

Third, despite the current Anglo-Saxon amnesia about Hegel and the turning of him into a stereotypical (and somewhat outdated) polemical target on the European continent, his logic has never enjoyed greater success, both among intellectuals and in the general population. People who would consider many of his specific theses laughable don't seem to be able to think any other way. Indeed, fragments of dialectical logic have been reinvented constantly, under different names of course: they have resurfaced as genealogies, chains of symbolic displacements, or family resemblances—and in fact I will find it profitable to use one of these simpler reformulations below. So it is this logic that constitutes what most matters about Hegel today.

With this third way of articulating what is crucial about Hegel's logic I have intersected the second driving force that has given this book its shape. For, clearly, many will disagree with my claim that Hegel is so immensely popular; and a good strategy for understanding the nature of the disagreement consists in asking about the frame of reference of that claim. Immensely popular, that is, with respect to what?

There is a battle of gods unfolding in the background of the (sometimes distinguished, sometimes petty) confrontations staged by the philosophy of the last two centuries, and structuring all such confrontations: the one between Kant and Hegel. At stake in this battle is the very relevance of philosophical work: is the philosopher, that is, entitled to pass a judgment on what is the case, to call it in question and criticize it, to elaborate utopian alternatives to it? Is there a conceptual place for values, and specifically moral values, in a world of facts? Or is any commitment to such values just another fact, characteristic of those curious but still perfectly determined creatures belonging to the species *homo sapiens*? In the wake of the inexorable necessitarianism issuing from most enthusiastic participants in the enterprise of the new science, Kant made a heroic effort to find such a place and located in the "ought (not) to," which gives the logical form of a value judgment, the highest dignity of human beings. Hegel's dialectical logic provided an enormously pliable, efficient, and seductive instrument that promised to forever bankrupt that effort and disqualify all value-talk as pathetic wishful thinking.

There has been resistance against the seduction, to be sure; but, by and large, it has not been very successful. As a result, utopian thinking is considered today an unfashionable, naive, even childish activity; ethics is being swallowed by either history or rational decision theory; the possibility of any agency that does not reduce to the spinning out of one's preference profile or to the staring at the unconcealment of being is highly doubtful. Nothing seems to be granted intellectual stature other than a complacent retrospective look—even when it is a look into one's future, which one will only respectably talk about insofar as it is one's past speaking.

I am with Kant. But, aside from the deep admiration I feel for his rival (though not for many of the latter's ungrateful heirs), I think that nothing is more dangerous for the cause I identify with than ignorance of the enemy's weapons. For it is precisely that ignorance which lets them exercise a more subterrenean and ultimately more influential action. So, I conclude, a book on Hegel is very much in order: it should focus on Hegel's logic and should oppose this logic as it accounts for it. How does a book do that? By opposing the comprehensiveness, the integral unity, the self-referentiality that "naturally" go with its subject matter. By being brief and "abstract"; by setting this be-all-and-end-all structure against *another* (!) one; by picking and choosing what matters and what doesn't, what we might want to use and what we might not. And by avoiding involvement with unnecessary "scholarship": by making a clear statement of it, so that everyone can recognize what the issue *and the danger* are.

This is (briefly put) why I thought I had to write a book about Hegel, and had to write it as I did. Will I ever give voice to those other resonances his texts conjured up in me, realize any of the other phantoms that occupied my fancy? Probably not. Pace Hegel, I am no infinite spirit; and how I choose to spend my limited time is how I substantiate my values. And, however attractive those prospects often are, there is too much else I judge worthier.

ONE

EQUIVOCAL WORDS

The first paragraph of the Aristotelian corpus is a definition of equivocality[1]:

> When things have only a name in common and the definition of being which corresponds to the name is different, they are called *homonymous*. Thus, for example, both a man and a picture are animals. These have only a name in common and the definition of being which corresponds to the name is different; for if one is to say what being an animal is for each of them, one will give two distinct definitions. (*Cat.* 3)[2]

One might wonder about this incipit—whether it is just accidental or some deep moral is supposed to be drawn from it. I believe the latter, and justifying this belief is the purpose of the present chapter.

1. Words and meanings

Logic is usually defined as a theory of valid inference. But an inference, valid or otherwise, is a system of meaningful linguistic expressions, and whether or not it is valid depends on what the meanings of those expressions are; so before we even know what validity is, and what logic (allegedly) is about, we must have a semantic theory— a theory of what sort of thing a meaning is, and how bits of language (come to) have such things. Otherwise put, logic as a theory of valid inference rests on a deeper sense of what logic is: logic as semantics.

6

According to Aristotle, there are two kinds of elementary meaningful (linguistic) expressions—that is, meaningful expressions whose meanings do not result from combining the meanings of their (meaningful) parts. They are names and verbs:

> A *name* is a spoken sound significant by convention, without time, none of whose parts is significant in separation. . . . A *verb* is what additionally signifies time, no part of it being significant separately; and it is a sign of things said of something else. (*De Int.* 25–26)[3]

Definitions, in one sense of *this* word,[4] provide accounts of what elementary meaningful expressions mean (or signify—the two words are used interchangeably here):

> Since a definition is said to be an account of what a thing is, it is evident that one type will be an account of what the name, or a different name-like account, signifies—e.g. what triangle signifies. (*Post. An.* 154)

> If what is signified by the name and by the account are not the same, clearly the account given will not be a definition. (*Topics* 257)

> The formula, of which the word is a sign, becomes its definition. (*Met.* 1598)

And definitions are constructed by first separating a class of entities (a genus) from other classes, and then separating the entity to be defined from the others belonging to the same class (through the differentia):

> For the genus ought to divide the object from other things, and the differentia from any of the things contained in the same genus. (*Topics* 237)

Summarizing this standard fare by way of an example gives us the following: "Man" is a name, that is, an elementary untensed meaningful expression. "Man is rational animal" is a definition of "man," that is, an account of what "man" means. So what "man" means is rational animal, that is, what is meant by the complex (untensed) meaningful expression "rational animal." And in general what any elementary meaningful expression means is what is meant by a certain collection of (other[5]) such expressions; that is, it is a certain collection of traits.[6]

A number of important conditions must be satisfied by the traits referred to in a definition. They must not be redundant, for instance (see *Topics* 236ff), and must be better known than what is being de-

fined (see *Topics* 238ff). But we can disregard such matters here and
focus on the most basic structure of a definition: on the fact that a
definition identifies the meaning of a linguistic expression as a stable
entity, in a (stable) relation of opposition with other similar entities.
Man is rational animal, period, and, if an animal is a living being that
has sensation and a plant is one that does not,[7] then an impassable
barrier exists between man and plant: part of what it is to be man
(and part of what "man" means) is to be set in a radical, irreducible
contrast to any plant. If anything that counts as man were to become
a plant, it would automatically *cease* to be man.

All of these stable Aristotelian meanings could ideally be represented in a universal tree of Porphyry (a dead tree, I take it, because
live trees are not that stable), or better a universal (petrified?) forest
of Porphyry, since there will be a tree corresponding to each category.
Each node of each such tree other than the very last ones (corresponding to the *infimae species*) is divided by a use of negation,[8] and
there is no going back on this division: once the node *corporeal substance* has been divided into *animate* and *inanimate*, and you have gone
(say) down the first branch, you have irretrievably lost the second
one, and all the part of the tree originating from it. To paraphrase
Bishop Butler, you now are what you are, *and not another thing*.

Within this framework, homonymy is an irritating source of confusion. If it turns out that "a sharp note is a swift note, . . . whereas
a sharp angle is one that is less than a right angle" (*Topics* 178), then
clearly people may be fooled when they use one and the same word
"sharp." They may think they are expressing the same meaning while
they are not, or take themselves to be arguing against each other while
they are in fact talking past each other: "an expression having more
than one use makes what is said unclear, because the man who is
about to attempt an argument is in doubt which of the various uses
the expression has" (*Topics* 218).[9] And, besides being victims of such
confusion and of the resulting fallacies, they may also go one step
further and make use of it in the intentional building of deceitful
arguments, to the effect (say) "that the mouse must be a noble creature, since it gives its name to the most august of all religious rites"
(*Rhetoric* 2233). Aristotle, by the way, is not too fussy about occasionally recommending this strategy:

> If a term be used in several ways, and it has been laid down that it
> belongs or that it does not belong to something, you should prove
> your case of one of its several uses, if you cannot prove it of both.

This rule is to be observed in cases where the difference of use is undetected. (*Topics* 183)

But, in general, homonymy is an enemy for him. An enemy to be faced firmly ("since the right of drawing the distinction [among the various senses of an equivocal word] is granted, one should not hesitate," *Soph. Ref.* 299) and cautiously ("it is not proper to give an unqualified answer to any homonymous question, not even if the predicate is true of all the subjects, as some claim that one should," *Soph. Ref.*). And, most important, a cunning enemy, one that "creeps in without being noticed" (*Topics* 179) and "sometimes pass[es] unobserved" (*Topics* 249); hence one that must be patiently, diligently, ingeniously uncovered if we are to deprive it of its pernicious influence. *Topics* 176–79 runs through a whole bag of tricks to be used against this furtive fiend: Check the contraries of different uses of a word—if here we find the contrary of "sharp" to be "flat" and there to be "dull," then those uses are infected with homonymy.[10] See if one use has an intermediate (as "clear" and "obscure" have in the case of colors) and another one does not (as seems to be true for those same words in the case of sounds). Examine the inflected forms—"if 'justly' is used in more than one way, the 'just,' also, will be used in more than one way." And on and on: multiple weapons are badly needed when the opposition can so effectively disguise itself.

Thus we have a first resolution for our initial wonder. Equivocal words are ubiquitous in ordinary language and make the use of it for scientific inquiry highly suspicious; hence before we get involved in such inquiry we need to alert our fellow searchers (and ourselves) to the danger and offer strategies for identifying and defusing this time bomb—or it will blow up in our face when we least need it, when we find ourselves leaning on a definition or an enthymeme that suddenly gives way.

And yet, this resolution is not enough to make the perplexity evaporate. For one continues to be puzzled about that very ubiquitous character we just found equivocality to have. Why would it have to be the case that this phenomenon is so common—and so deeply entrenched in our forms of speech? If indeed "spoken sounds are symbols of affections in the soul, and written marks symbols of spoken sounds" (*De Int.* 25), why are those sounds and marks so consistently misleading? Why do they make it so easy to fall into the trap of addressing someone's word *as opposed to* his thought—which is what happens "whenever a man does not use the word in the sense about

which the person being questioned thought he was being questioned"
(*Soph. Ref.* 289)? Is it a coincidence that such an unfortunate situation
arises so often? Is it perhaps a degeneration of the "true nature" of
language? But "the nature of things is the nature which most of them
possess for most of the time" (*On the Heavens* 493[11]); hence this regular
occurrence, however disturbing, cannot be a product of chance.
There must be something in language, in the very nature of it, that
invites equivocality and is responsible for its constantly getting in the
way of serious intellectual work. And what could that be?

2. Universals

No equivocality would ever occur if the radical course were taken of
always assigning different names to different things. But, though Aristotle admits that "it may sometimes be necessary even to invent
names, if no name exists in relation to which a thing would be given
properly" (*Cat.* 11)[12], in general this course is impossible: "names are
finite and so is the sum-total of accounts, while things are infinite in
number. Inevitably, then, the same account and a single name signify
several things" (*Soph. Ref.* 278). A language of proper names would
not be an effective tool in dealing with the whole wide world: infinitely many elements of it would remain out of reach. Linguistic
economy is a necessity: we need to refer to things wholesale if
things—lots of them—are not to escape us altogether. In addition to
individuals, we must be able to name *universals*, where "by the universal we mean that which is predicable of the individuals" (*Met.*
1579), that is, "a kind of whole" (*Physics* 315), something that "belong[s] to more than one subject" (*Parts* 1003) or "naturally belongs
to more than one thing" (*Met.* 1639).

Nor is it just a matter of numbers: reference to universals is also
needed if language is to help bring about any genuine epistemic contact with the world. For "men do not think they know a thing till
they have grasped the 'why' of it (which is to grasp its primary cause)"
(*Physics* 332), and to grasp that is to grasp a necessary connection,
which is required to have understanding: "that of which there is understanding *simpliciter* [that is, *proper* understanding, as opposed to what
can occur accidentally in the sophistic fashion] cannot be otherwise"
(*Post. An.* 115).[13] But necessity is not to be found at the level of
individual things or events: at that level, we can only observe what
is or happens, but we don't even have the machinery to address the

issue of what *has to* be or happen. For that machinery to be in place, universals must be brought in: one must disengage oneself from concrete spatiotemporal occurrences and contemplate their eternal structure—that is, contemplate what is universal in them.

> Nor can one understand through perception. For even if perception is of what is such and such, and not of individuals, still one necessarily perceives an individual and at a place and at a time, and it is impossible to perceive what is universal and holds in every case; for that is not an individual not at a time; for then it would not be universal—for it is what is always and everywhere that we call universal. . . . If we were on the moon and saw the earth screening it we would not know the explanation of the eclipse. For we would perceive that it is eclipsed and not why at all; for there turned out to be no perception of the universal. (*Post. An.* 144)

Similarly, "the object of knowledge is of necessity" (*Nic. Eth.* 1799), and hence "the knowledge of anything is universal" (*Met.* 1584[14]). For, again, knowledge and understanding are intimately related: "to know what something is and to know the explanation of the fact that it is are the same" (*Post. An.* 153), which is why "it is not enough for a definitional account to express as most now do the mere fact; it must include and exhibit the cause also" (*On the Soul* 657–58). And indeed, not only is any cognitive approach intrinsically a universal one: we should also be constantly striving to make our cognitive practices more so—since to know more generally, it seems, is to know better.

> You should . . . always examine arguments to see whether they rest on principles of general application; for all particular arguments reason universally as well, and a particular demonstration always contains a universal demonstration, because it is impossible to deduce at all without using universals. (*Topics* 277)

So there are two basic reasons why our language must name universals: because otherwise (a) it could not talk about the whole world and (b) it could not provide any cognitive access to it. But note that (b) is a more restrictive reason than (a). Something could be a "universal" on the basis of (a) if it just gathered a bunch of individuals *somehow or other;* whereas something counts as a universal satisfying (b) only if it carves nature at its joints—that is, if by grouping individuals together in the way it does it also reveals some of the necessary laws that regulate their behavior. "Universal attributes belong to things in virtue of their own nature" (*Met.* 1607).[15]

To articulate the same point differently, a definition is "always universal" (*Post. An.* 161) and "of the universal" (*Met.* 1636)—which also accounts for why "we have never yet become aware of anything by giving a definition" (*Post. An.* 149). But if (a) were all the reason we had for universals, definitions could be very liberally conceived: any laundry list would do, "one could posit a name for any account whatever, . . . and the *Iliad* would be a definition" (*Post. An.* 153). (b), however, forces us to be far more demanding: "a definition is a formula which is one not by being connected together, like the *Iliad*,[16] but by dealing with one object" (*Met.* 1650). "A definition is a phrase signifying a thing's essence" (*Topics* 169[17]), since the essence of a thing, what makes it the *one* thing it is, is also what the thing *necessarily* is— and that is what universals need to bring out if they are to be serviceable in cognitive contexts.

Gathering things under one label is a trivial operation, and one for which there are virtually no criteria of success or failure: to attempt it is automatically to succeed. But gathering things in such a way as to reveal their essence—the rational structure that makes it possible for us to understand (and know) how they could not be other than they are—is quite a different accomplishment, and one that requires constant attention and keen logical sense[18]: "it is the easiest of all things to demolish a definition, while to establish one is the hardest" (*Topics* 260). It is a process of constantly finetuning the adjustment between words and world. Sometimes essences have no names attached to them:

> There is . . . no one term to denote all animals that have a lung; no designation, that is, like the term bird, applicable to the whole of a certain class. Yet the possession of a lung is a part of their substance, just as much as the presence of certain characters constitutes the essence of a bird. (*Parts* 1043–44)

At other times we have the name but are missing some of the terms we need to articulate the account, so we need to add them to our vocabulary:

> The citizen whom we are seeking to define is a citizen in the strictest sense, . . . and his special characteristic is that he shares in the administration of justice, and in offices. Now of offices some are discontinuous, and the same persons are not allowed to hold them twice, or can only hold them after a fixed interval; others have no limit of time—for example, the office of juryman or member of the assembly. It may, indeed, be argued that these are not magistrates at all, and that

their functions give them no share in the government. But surely it is ridiculous to say that those who have the supreme power do not govern. Let us not dwell further upon this, which is a purely verbal question; what we want is a common term including both juryman and member of the assembly. Let us . . . call it "indefinite office," and we will assume that those who share in such office are citizens. This is the most comprehensive definition of a citizen, and best suits all those who are generally so called. (*Politics* 2023–24)

And at yet other times we face competing accounts of the same name and have to decide which is better:

Our definition is best adapted to the citizen of a democracy. . . . We may . . . modify our definition of the citizen so as to include these [other] states. (*Politics* 2024)

It is within the space existing between these two distinct operations—trivial gathering as such and the cognitively relevant gathering that exposes the world's joints—that homonymy can prosper and display all of its confusing power. For, clearly, some sounds and some angles can be grouped together by using the word "sharp"; but, if one were then to rely on the deceptive unity thus created to explain why, say, hitting the sharp edge of a certain piece of furniture produces a certain note, one would be deluding oneself. So it is crucial to point out that a universal is "some one and the same thing, *nonhomonymous*, holding of several cases" (*Post. An.* 125; italics mine) and that "one who knows universally knows . . . better . . . than one who knows . . . particularly" *provided that such "universal knowledge" is not a case of homonymy* (*Post. An.* 140).

Homonymy is thus, in the Aristotelian scheme of things, a main occupational hazard of scientific activity: insofar as the latter must concern itself with universals and be expressed in universal terms, it forever runs the risk of seeing such universalities explode—prove to be fatuous connections, of no explanatory value whatsoever. "For homonymies escape notice in what is universal more," hence in "proceed[ing] . . . to what is common" among several particulars one must always "[take] care not to fall into homonymy" (*Post. An.* 162).[19]

On the basis of this discussion, one can certainly think of the identification of proper universals as work in progress—indeed, even as work never to be completed but always asymptotically tending to a perfect fit between linguistic and ontological structures. What one has *prima facie* more trouble considering plausible is the idea that Aristotle would be perfectly reconciled with several—indeed, virtually all—of his fundamental terms having multiple uses for which no single definition could be provided. But this is indeed, famously, the case. " 'Is' is used in many ways," we read at *Physics* 316, and the same claim is repeated over and over again throughout the corpus.[20] "Non-being" has as many senses as "being" does (*Met.* 1721[21]); and an analogous multiplicity affects "one" (*Physics* 317), "sameness" (*Soph. Ref.* 286), and "good" (*Nic. Eth.* 1732). The whole book V of the *Metaphysics* is a painstaking analysis of how much multiplicity of meaning is hidden in such basic terms as "origin," "cause," "element," "nature," and "necessary." So the question is bound to arise, how can this be? Specifically, how can there be "a science which investigates being as being" (*Met.* 1584), when "being" has no univocity to it—so much so that "what is is not a genus" (*Post. An.* 152[22])? How can there be any interesting generalizations for this science to make, when being applies unqualifiedly to everything—when its semantics seems to be the mother of all laundry lists?

> Since the science of the philosopher treats of being *qua* being universally and not of some part of it, and "being" has many senses and is not used in one only, it follows that if it is used homonymously and in virtue of no common nature, it does not fall under one science. (*Met.* 1676)

To answer these questions we must return to the beginning of the corpus: to the fact that "homonymous" and its (apparent) contradictory "synonymous" (which is what things are called when they "have the name in common and the definition of being which corresponds to the name is the same," *Cat.* 3) are supplemented there by a third word that does not seem to operate at the same level, and yet is defined in the same breath with them—the three definitions indeed constitute the whole first section of this first Aristotelian treatise.

> When things get their name from something, with a difference of ending, they are called *paronymous*. Thus, for example, the grammarian gets his name from grammar, the brave get theirs from bravery. (*Cat.* 3)

3. Focal meanings

Words are not isolated: they belong to complex families where meanings are related in subtle, and often systematic, ways. We know already that we can use these networks to learn about their members—that the equivocality of an adverb can be indicative of a coordinated phenomenon affecting the relevant adjective, say. But there is more to paronymy than that; to see what it is, we need to make an important digression.

What makes a word a word—as opposed to an inkblot or a sound—is that it has meaning: "each word is a symbol" (*Sense* 694), and, as we already know, "words express ideas" (*Rhetoric* 2250) and through them "represent things" (*Rhetoric* 2239). Though Aristotle does not make this point specifically for words, it is easy to extrapolate from what he says about pictures and images[23] that treating a word *as a word* amounts to conferring on it a different ontological status than treating it as an ordinary object—that is, to centering that status around its "standing for" role rather than (say) any perceptual quality it might have.

But then it follows that what makes a word the particular word it is—what gives it its identity *as a word*—is what particular meaning it has, what particular idea/thing it stands for; so we cannot really make sense of *one* word having multiple meanings. We might make sense of different meanings being associated with the same inkblot or sound; but, when it comes to words, different meanings must be conveyed by different vehicles. Common parlance here is not helpful: when equivocality is in question, we typically talk as if indeed one and the same word were used in different ways. Such language, however, is misleading: equivocality is more properly described by saying that *two* (or more) words are indistinguishable as twins are, written and spoken in the same way, but still absolutely distinct. Because of a word's dual status, we will inevitably fall back into talking about one word standing for different ideas/things, meaning by "word" the perceptually identifiable configuration the word *also* is; but if necessary we can always set the matter right by having different such configurations correspond to the different, specifically *word*like roles they play.

> It makes no difference even if one were to say a word has several meanings, if only they are limited in number; for to each formula there might be assigned a different word. For instance, we might say that "man" has not one meaning but several, one of which would be defined as "two-footed animal," while there might be also several other formulae if only they were limited in number; for a special name might be assigned to each of the formulae. (*Met.* 1589[24])

The digression is now at an end, and we are in a position to notice that paronymy is a phenomenon of far greater significance and depth than its somewhat casual introduction might suggest. For families of related words might well contain several different replicas of "the same" word: (some of) the different meanings of "sharp," say, might be coordinated with one another as the meanings of "just" and "justly" are[25]—(some of) the different words indistinguishably pronounced and written "sharp" might display as much of a relation of dependence on one another as an adjective has with the corresponding noun (or vice versa).

> Everything which is healthy is related to health, one thing in the sense that it preserves health, another in the sense that it produces it, another in the sense that it is a symptom of health, another because it is capable of it. And that which is medical is relative to the medical art, one thing in the sense that it possesses it, another in the sense that it is naturally adapted to it, another in the sense that it is a function of the medical art. And we shall find other words used similarly to these. (*Met.* 1584)

Thus paronymy gives Aristotle a tool for handling the threat of indiscriminate fragmentation to which his whole conception of logic and science is exposed. For there is a third possibility now, in addition to meanings simply being identical or distinct: they can be *correlated*, and "it belongs in all cases to one and the same science to deal with correlated subjects" (*Parts* 998). Hence in particular there can be a science of being as being because all the multiple senses of being come together in an organized way.

> There are many senses in which a thing may be said to "be," but they are related to one central point, one definite kind of thing, and they are not homonymous. . . . All refer to one starting-point; some things are said to be because they are substances, others because they are affections of substance, others because they are a process toward substance, or destructions or privations or qualities of substance, or productive or generative of substance, or of things which are relative to substance, or negations of some of these things or of substance itself. (*Met.* 1584)[26]

> A term belongs to different sciences not if it has different senses, but if its definitions neither are identical nor can be referred to one central meaning. (*Met.* 1586)

In articulating this approach further, it will be useful to distinguish two aspects of it. To begin with, most multiple meanings of "the same" word are not random: typically, words are not just assigned to different sites in the forest of Porphyry out of sheer perversity. There is a method to this madness. Most often, the reason why a word is stretched to cover more than one definitional account is that there are no words available for certain accounts (once again, our resources are limited) and hence, rather than just making up new ones, words in the vicinity are adapted to new tasks.

> This is what ripening means when the word is applied to fruit. However, many other things that have undergone concoction are said to be ripe, the general character of the process being the same, though the word is applied by an extension of meaning. The reason for this extension is . . . that the various modes in which natural heat and cold perfect the matter they determine have not special names appropriated to them. (*Meteor.* 610[27])

So, for example, various kinds of people who are not, strictly speaking, brave are called brave "by an extension of the word" (*Nic. Eth.* 1760), and the name "self-indulgence" is applied by "transference" to childish faults (*Nic. Eth.* 1767), and a man may be considered a friend to himself "by analogy, not absolutely" (*Eud. Eth.* 1965).[28] In all such cases, semantic drift is at work: by metaphor or metonymy, words acquire "figurative" or "extended" meanings, and in general a story can be told on how such figures or extensions were generated on the basis of what was "originally" there.[29]

But drifting away, all by itself, will not do: it will not guarantee the kind of unity that is necessary for a universal term to have epistemic value—and for a science utilizing that term to be *one* science. The last passage from *Met.* 1584 quoted above suggests that there can be a doctrine of being not just because the various senses of "being" are related *somehow or other*, but because they are neatly arranged *around a center*. There is a primary sense of "being," also called a "focal meaning" for it—being as substance—and every other sense of the word *depends upon* the primary one: it *is* a sense of "being" *because* of the dependence relation that what it applies to has to what the primary sense applies to. There is definitely a head to the "being" household, a central star for this system, and that is what makes it possible for a single discipline to be devoted to its study. The same is true—indeed, *must* be true—for any number of other key concepts.

> Even if 'one' has several meanings, the other meanings will be related to the primary meaning. (*Met.* 1587)

From what has been said, . . . it is plain that nature in the primary and strict sense is the substance of things, which have in themselves, as such, a source of movement. (*Met.* 1603)

Quality . . . seems to have practically two meanings, and one of these is the more proper. (*Met.* 1611)

There are several kinds of friendship—firstly and in the proper sense that of good men *qua* good, and by similarity the other kinds. (*Nic. Eth.* 1829)

When carefully analyzed, however, this solution can be seen to raise residual, serious difficulties. Let us recapitulate: The basis of our original problem was that universals are supposed to fulfill two distinct functions, linguistic economy and explanatory use, and there is no reason to think that what fulfills the first function should also fulfill the second one. We can group together all sorts of things (indeed, *all* things) by saying that they *are*, and it might be the case that by doing so we learn absolutely nothing (or, worse still, deceive ourselves) about them, because "being" is a term with no unity to it. Faced by the danger that anything we took to be a universal might thus explode into a proliferation of clones, we developed the notion of meanings being parasitical on one another; but for this notion to be of any help parasitical meanings must, once more, display two distinct features— they must be derived from one another by semantic drift *and also* related to one another as planets are to a single sun. And it is an empirical matter whether anything that has the first feature also has the second. That any specific account be an explanation, then, depends on the truth of the empirical conjecture that the terms mobilized in it have meanings with the properly centered structure—and the same will hold for any system of accounts that presents itself as a scientific discipline. It is, again, just an empirical fact (when it is) that a given convoluted story of transferred meanings circles around a privileged point; and, if it doesn't, paronymy will collapse into homonymy and the relevant "universal" will testify to no regularity whatsoever. That is, something will happen to our explanations which is similar to what happens to noses in the passage below:

A nose which varies from the ideal of straightness to a hook or snub may still be of good shape and agreeable to the eye; but if the excess is very great, all symmetry is lost, and the nose at last ceases to be a nose at all on account of some excess in one direction or defect in the other; and this is true of every other part of the human body. (*Politics* 2079)[30]

But this means that we have not really exorcised homonymy: that it continues to haunt us. For how can we be sure that the meaning of "being," say, really has the centered structure we need? Have we examined *all* of its uses, in *all* contexts? And what happens if our cunning enemy is still hidden somewhere? What sense would our "science of being as being" make then? In general, how do we know that we have enough properly centered universals available to successfully carry out any scientific enterprise? The earlier innocent-sounding suggestion that the finding of adequate universals might be destined to remain work in progress has grown into the monumental threat that we might never know that we have enough of these universals even to get started.

Particularly troublesome in this regard are those cases where a phenomenon is exactly intermediate between two distinct (and, we may assume, properly centered) constellations of meaning, and each constellation has an equally legitimate claim to "extending" over it—thus implicitly challenging the unity of the other (if it is essential to an *A* that it be not-*B*, how about these *A*s that seem to *B*s as well?). And there are cases like that, which suggests the disturbing possibility that, when they do not arise, it is entirely contingent that they do not and scientific generalizations might depend for their meaningfulness on the fortunate circumstance that no such phenomena have yet arisen— or on the tragically *un*fortunate circumstance that they have not yet come to our attention.

> Nature proceeds little by little from things lifeless to animal life in such a way that it is impossible to determine the exact line of demarcation, nor on which side thereof an intermediate form should lie. (*Hist. of An.* 922)

> The sea-anemones . . . lie outside the recognized groups. Their constitution approximates them on one side to plants, on the other to animals. (*Parts* 1062)

Occasionally Aristotle suggests dealing with such trouble by a strategy to whose significance I will return later—that is, by *blaming* it on degeneration.[31] But a value judgment is not enough: it continues to be the case that (a) universals are needed to speak the world; (b) synonymous uses of (presumed) universals are by no means the rule; (c) homonymous uses of universals provide no (or, even worse, delusional) understanding; (d) for non-synonymous uses of universals to have cognitive value, they must be arranged around a focal meaning;

and (e) it is an open question how far this arrangement reaches with any specific universal.

In conclusion, it seems that Aristotle's semantic theory puts understanding, explanation, knowledge, and science on shaky grounds. Shall we try to fix it?[32] Shall we learn to live with the shakiness? Or shall we explore a different tack altogether?

TWO

A SEMANTICS OF NARRATIVES

In the preface to the second edition of Hegel's *Science of Logic* we read the following:

> Some . . . [German] words . . . possess the . . . peculiarity of having not only different but opposite meanings so that one cannot fail to recognize a speculative spirit of the language in them: it can delight a thinker to come across such words and to find the union of opposites naively shown in the dictionary as one word with opposite meanings, although this result of speculative thinking is nonsensical to the understanding. (32)[1]

There could no more striking opposition on this matter than the one surfacing here between Aristotle ("the deepest and also the most comprehensive thinker of antiquity," *History* 272[2]) and Hegel: whereas the former felt equivocality to be a source of embarrassment, an imperfection to be repaired, an unfortunate accident that threatened the very substance of his (or anyone's) scientific work, the latter rejoices at its occurrence, finds it to be evidence that language is telling us something of great "speculative" significance, indeed it is more of a joy for him (and more significant) if words have not only distinct but also contradictory meanings—and we will see that one of his most crucial philosophical terms "suffers" precisely from such a "predicament." So, what exactly is going on here? How can a word's oxymoronic vicissitudes reveal something so intrinsically valuable?

1. Potential and actual

Besides focal meaning, Aristotle has another strategy available for handling homonymy. It is not fully worked out, and is ultimately unsatisfactory; but it will put us on the right track. It surfaces most clearly in the *Metaphysics*, where he must face squarely the unwelcome fact that the universal character of language (and explanation) is not limited to those words which are most obviously universal because they bear their grouping, gathering character on their sleeve—predicates, that is. A proper name like "Socrates" works in much the same way: there are all sorts of spacetime slices "falling under" it, and there is the same danger here as everywhere of seeing that collection trivialized, reduced to a jumbled-up mess with nothing but verbal unity to it. Or, conversely (and adapting words from Hegel), "a large and ancient tree puts out more and more branches without thereby becoming a new tree" (*Right* 249); but how shall we understand this identity in difference?

Thus the most general problem of the *Metaphysics* is that of accounting for the identity of spatiotemporal continuants. One can attempt to find some "essence" that remains unchanged through all their various incidents, but, if this is what their identity is based on, it is likely to make Socrates indistinguishable from Plato (or Callicles and Thrasimachus, for that matter). A more appealing strategy is to think that each later phase of Socrates is unfolding the promise contained in previous phases—that Socrates is progressively realizing, *actualizing* what he was *potentially*.[3] Socrates the little child can be conceived as the *matter* which later was to flourish and take shape (or *form*) as Socrates the adolescent and the mature man—and that matter could only take such a shape because it had it implicitly in itself, because it was *possible* for it to grow that way: "the actuality of any given thing can only be realized in what is already potentially that thing, i.e. in a matter of its own appropriate to it" (*On the Soul* 659).[4]

Part of what makes this approach a failure is how inarticulate Aristotle is when it comes to accounting for the ontological relation between potential and actual. He is convinced that potential-X and actual-X are identical but is not prepared to say why—indeed he claims that one cannot say it, that what we are looking at is a pair of primitive concepts.

People look for a unifying formula, and a difference, between potentiality and actuality. But . . . the proximate matter and the form are one and the same thing, the one potentially, the other actually. Therefore to ask the cause of their being one is like asking the cause of unity in general; for each thing is a unity, and the potential and the actual are somehow one. (*Met.* 1650–51)

Actuality means the existence of the thing, not in the way which we express by "potentially." . . . Our meaning can be seen in the particular cases by induction, and we must not seek a definition of everything but be content to grasp the analogy. (*Met.* 1655)

However, such speechlessness is a ruse (not necessarily intended, of course). For let us review the main steps: Our problem is how Socrates-at-t_1 can be one and the same thing as Socrates-at-t_2, as opposed to their being two distinct things equivocally referred to by "the same" name. The alleged solution of the problem is to claim that, though Socrates-at-t_1 has different properties from Socrates-at-t_2, the former is-potentially what the latter is-actually, and being-potentially is "somehow" the same as being-actually. But then whether this is in any way a solution for our problem depends on how the "somehow" is cashed out; specifically, if the relation between being-potentially and being-actually is one of homonymy, we are back where we started. We may have reduced all distinct cases of homonymy to one (at least as far as spatiotemporal continuants are concerned), but the substance of our problem remains the same. Therefore, for this approach to be successful, the burden is on Aristotle to prove that more than homonymy is at issue.

But he does not dispose of the burden. The best conjecture we can make, from the little he says about the matter, is that this might be another case of paronymy—with being-actual as the focal meaning. And even that is at most an opaque claim, not a convincingly elaborated one.

"Being" is in one way divided into "what," quality, and quantity, and is in another way distinguished in respect of potentiality and fulfillment. (*Met.* 1651)

Clearly . . . [actuality] is prior in formula; for that which is in the primary sense potential is potential because it is possible for it to become actual. (*Met.* 1657)[5]

This is where Aristotle leaves it. But it is an interesting suggestion: it makes us think of an identity that overcomes the rigid, *and static,* definitional framework in which we have moved so far—an identity compatible with, maybe even constituted by, dramatic change. And it invites us to speculate that such a dynamic identity might take care not only of the implicitly universal names of spatiotemporal continuants, but of explicit universals as well—of unity as such, which is what makes a universal. This is the road we have to travel now, to get to Hegel's side of the equation.

2. Family resemblances

Let us start small, and in some other land.[6] Suppose you are looking at a picture of several members of the Brown family, and from looking at it you derive a strong sense of the identity of this family—and of how such an identity is sharply distinct from that of, say, the Smith family. Suppose you are asked to articulate what the identity amounts to: to specify the semantics of the expression "the Brown family" (within the confines provided by the picture). It won't do to abstract from the Brown family members to something (some traits) that they all have in common and that would jointly provide a definition of what it is to be one of them: most likely, this "essence" of the Brown family will be (as in the previous case of the essence of Socrates) so vague as to coincide with the essence of the Smith family. With both, you are going to come down to trivial matters such as having a mouth and two eyes, legs and arms and a torso. Nor will it do to go the way suggested by paronymy and focal meaning, that is, to look for someone in the picture whom everyone else clearly resembles (more than they resemble any of the Smiths, say), however dissimilar *from one another* they might be; for, again, you might well not find any such person. A more promising course is to consider someone *A* in the picture and point out that *A* obviously belongs to the same family as someone else *B* because of how closely they resemble each other; and then that *B* obviously belongs to the same family as *C* because of how closely *they* resemble each other; and so on. By the end, you may have reached someone *Z* who doesn't look at all like *A* but still belongs to the Brown family because of how closely he resembles the person who immediately precedes him in this trajectory. And then you can say that it is the trajectory itself, the path leading you from *A* to *Z*, that constitutes the meaning of the expression "the Brown family," *not* any definite collection of traits.

A lot of work will have to be done to spell out exactly what kind of thing we expect a "trajectory" or a "path" to be. The first bit we will do right away, and in doing it we will also get ready to pretty much kiss the very terms "trajectory" and "path" goodbye; for, though there is nothing in principle wrong with them, they do convey misleading associations. Whatever the case may be with Wittgenstein, according to the heuristic use I am making here of family resemblances the meaning of the expression "the Brown family" is not (simply) a certain ordering of the members of that family: it is (also) inclusive of the accounts "connecting" each member with the adjacent ones—for example the one pointing out that Tom and Sybil must definitely be related because of what their lips and ears look like. So, if "trajectory" and "path" suggest that there be nothing more to what these terms refer to than a (one-dimensional) line going from A to B to C . . . , then it's best to drop them: the "line" must have a lot of structure, carry a lot of information. A more effective way of conveying the right associations would be to say that the semantics of "the Brown family" is the *story* (or *narrative*) which takes one from A to B to C . . . , and thereby establishes that they are members of the same family. (And, of course, one can then go on talking about trajectories and paths if *that* is what one means by it.)

Let us generalize. As I pointed out earlier, the pervasiveness of equivocal words can be attributed to semantic drift: originally, a word has a given meaning, but then, by metaphor or metonymy, that first meaning becomes associated with another, and the word acquires this second meaning as well. And so on. Often, when a word acquires a new meaning, (some of) the old ones recede into the background (become obsolete), but given the universal comprehensiveness of natural language they are not canceled (or maybe they are canceled and preserved at the same time: they are still there, but made largely inactive). In this picture, semantic drift is *external* to semantics (and logic in general): there is a theory of how words are assigned meanings and, quite independently, there is the (disturbing) empirical fact that the meanings words are assigned keep changing all of the time, thus forcing us to continually revise our semantic scheme—worse yet, to continually overimpose new semantic schemes over the old ones. In a first approximation to Hegel's picture, on the other hand, semantic drift becomes part of semantics: the history of a word becomes its meaning.[7] Or, to put it in the material mode, what it is to be the referent of that word becomes the same as having had that history.

If we are to describe what a body *is*, the whole cycle of its alterations must be stated; for the true individuality of body does not exist in a single state but is exhausted and displayed only in this cycle of states. (*Nature* 270)[8]

To refine this approximation somewhat, we go back to terminology and notice that two cognate—but still substantially different—words have been used in characterizing Hegel's position: "history" and "story." Which one best expresses what we are aiming at? As is most often the case when Hegel is in question, both do: they both bring out important (and conflicting) elements of his view. "History" signals that we are talking about something actual: meanings here are no creatures of fancy, no "forms" irrelevantly attached to some brute, existing "content." They are steeped in reality; indeed, they are what reality itself amounts to.[9] And yet, what is called upon should not be confused with chronological history. For there we are used to accepting all sorts of inconsequential absurdities just because "they happened," but this kind of happening Hegel would judge insignificant—and indeed untrue. In *Religion* II, for example, he berates the spectacles the Romans were fond of, where people (and animals) were in fact killed on the stage (or in the arena), and here is the specific form his condemnation takes:

> The spectators wanted to see not a spiritual history but one that was actually happening. . . . They wanted . . . [an] external, simple story of death, without meaning [!], the quintessence of everything external, the arid process of a *natural* death by violence or natural means, not death produced by an ethical power. (222)

What we are looking for is a demonstration, not a list of events,[10] and though eventually even chronological history will have to be redeemed that way—itself turned into a demonstration[11]—that is a much more complicated point than the texture of our current discussion can bear; so let us say for the moment that "story" is a better term for what we are talking about, that to begin with Hegel's semantics can be characterized as one of narratives, for it is narratives, stories, that words mean.

Through the remainder of the present chapter, I will highlight various consequences of this general approach, thus providing increasingly articulate versions of it. But, even at the present rudimentary stage of analysis, I am able to throw some light on why one might be "delighted" with words having distinct, indeed opposite, "meanings."

Suppose you are looking at a picture of the Adams family. It is a weird family: all of its twenty members are identical twins, they all seem to have popped into being out of thin air, and to have no offspring. There is certainly a story you can tell that connects them with one another; but it's a boring story, and insisting that that story be the semantics of "the Adams family," as opposed to a collection of the traits all the members have in common (which turn out to be *all* of their traits), would seem a case of ideologically motivated pedantry. Or suppose it is the Bates family you are looking at: its members are not identical, but they are close enough. Their hair is always some shade of blond, their eyes some gradation of blue, their bone structure tends to be massive. Maybe you cannot cluster them all around a single patriarch; but surely you can extrapolate from them to an ideal Bates, on whom all real ones could be seen as variations. And then the ideal specimen is all you need if you want to say what "being a Bates" means.

With the Browns it's different: as you tell the story that brings them together, you find yourself going from a blond beauty to some dark homely creature (because of their bone structure), and then from some sturdy fighter-type to a thin, delicate weakling (because of those ears), so much so that by the end you are assembling people who have absolutely nothing in common—whose every trait manifests radical dissimilarity. With the Browns, you know that you could never catch their family spirit *except through a story*: it's families like that which dispel the delusion one might have that a single (perhaps ideal) collection of traits will do the trick. I said before that something of this sort could happen with a family; what becomes apparent now is that it's best when it does—because it makes misunderstandings impossible.

Turning from pictures to words: Language is manifesting its structure in the clearest manner when the dictionary throws contradictory definitions at us. For then it is bringing out in the most obvious terms what we might well miss in less extreme circumstances. We should be grateful—and indeed happy—when what is otherwise mostly implicit strikes us so, with complete transparency. This is far from being all there is to Hegel's delight with the "speculative spirit of the language," but it's a good beginning.[12]

3. Concepts and the concept

So Hegel is highly appreciative of language, which he calls (at *Mind* 147) the "perfect expression" of spirit.[13] And indeed what he has to say could well be said in the linguistic terms so popular in contemporary philosophy; as we will see, there is nothing especially "mental" to concepts and thought for him.[14] But we will also see that he has a good reason for preferring a mentalistic jargon after all; so, instead of talking (directly) about the meanings of words here, we need to phrase our account in terms of the concepts those words express.

The Latinate word "concept" conveys a forgotten resonance of grasping, as does its German counterpart, "Begriff." A concept is, first and foremost, a universal, a one-over-many: a reaching out to what is distinct and a laboring to incorporate it into some kind of unity. Since language is the perfect expression of spirit, incidentally, there is nothing more to language than that very reaching out:

> Thought is itself and its other, . . . it overgrasps its other and . . . nothing escapes it. And because *language* is the work of thought, nothing can be said in language that is not universal. (*Logic* 50)[15]

So consider *A* and *B* in the picture of the Brown family. They are two distinct individuals, whom we can expect to have been born at different times and to live in different places, to be identified by different experiences and interests. In all sorts of ways, they are antagonistic to each other—one might say that they repel each other. But, by the time we have brought them both under the concept *member of the Brown family*, we have to some extent overcome their antagonism, found them to be elements of one and the same process: the "natural" development gradually taking us from *A* to *Z*, which is what that concept amounts to. In Hegelian terms, we have overcome the appearance that there be something ultimately *real* to these individuals, some irreducible residue to them, and brought out their *ideality*, their character as *ideal moments*: the fact that their distinctness is only the articulation of a fundamental unity.

> *Ideality* . . . [is] the reduction of the idea's otherness to a *moment*, the process of returning—and the accomplished return—into itself of the idea from its other. (*Mind* 9)[16]

But is this a legitimate way to put it? Does the fact that all sorts of distinct implements fall under the concept *table* entail any level of identification among them? Are we not simply confusing the "is" of predication with the "is" of identity when we suggest so?

As a first step toward answering such queries, consider how different a concept looks in the Aristotelian and the Hegelian frameworks—as elaborated so far. (Or, as Hegel would put it, how different it looks within the perspectives of divisive understanding and unifying reason.[17]) In the former, some specific collection of traits is abstracted—that is, separated—from a bunch of objects; which means that, from then on, those objects are set aside, let go, forgotten, and one concentrates on the abstracted collection. Once the latter is clearly circumscribed, there will be an indefinite number of objects (including, but not limited to, those originally abstracted from) to which it applies ("a host of particulars of outer existence and actions is embraced by a conception—battle, war, nation, ocean, or animal, for example," *Science* 34–35); but such application is irrelevant to what the concept is, and the abstraction process is immediately degraded to an "epistemic" mode of access to an august "logical" matter. The verso of this logical irrelevance of individuals is that logic will have no purchase on them—will not "grasp" them in their individuality. They will remain the real objects they are, really distinct from one another, and only marginally touched by the labeling we make of them on the basis of what properties they have. The danger that such groupings be purely contingent, that they reveal nothing of the objects' "essence," will be, as we have seen, an occupational hazard; but, even if that threat is successfully countered in any given case, the essence we have brought out will issue from a disregarding of precisely what opposes its various manifestations—precisely what would let us distinguish such manifestations from one another, identify them *as* individuals.

Within the narrative approach to conceptuality, on the other hand, no such separation occurs. It is indeed like telling a story—say the story of some character. In any one phase (ideal moment) of the story, the character is drawn in rich detail, and by the time he goes through some dramatic transformation he doesn't *lose* that detail, is not mortified into some pale sketch that only retains a portion of it—the portion common to his later phase. He will always *have had* the previous amount of detail, that is part of his history ("We'll always have Paris"), and to it he will *add* what else is now going on with him—however contradictory it might be to what was going on before. Everything happens here, so to speak, at ground level: we do not lose the individuality of an individual as we proceed from it to the next one, hence there is more credibility to the claim that the identity we are hereby establishing is the identity of distinct things ("identity in difference," indeed), not the analytic identity of one and the same structure being lifted from those distinct things and then repeating itself without change whenever the things are characterized as "instances" of it.[18]

But the story character per se will not suffice to establish that one's distinct individuality is "reduced" to a moment of a larger unity. For we can still think that there is more to any member of a family than being part of it—however elaborate and convincing an account we mean to include in the concept *member of the family*. The complexity of any such account is still consistent with the individual maintaining its character as a "real residue"—with its individuality not being fully grasped. It may well be that a character in a story (a "real" one) is entirely exhausted by what the story says, and that it would make no sense to ask questions about it that the story has no answers for; but is it in that sense (and here we are touching again the delicate issue of how this story can also be [a] history) that we can think of distinct *real* tables as exhausted by the concept *table*? Is there not a radical otherness in those real objects that is entirely indifferent to the conceptual detail we expose in thinking and talking about them? (Kant, for one, would certainly think so.[19])

To address the new worries, we need to make a second step: all of our talk of concepts so far was not accurate, since there are no concepts in the plural here—there is only one.

> It is false to speak of concepts of diverse sorts, for the concept as such, although concrete, is still essentially *one*, and the moments contained within it must not be considered to be diverse sorts of concepts. (*Logic* 245)

Language might be the perfect expression of spirit, but it does send confusing messages.[20] One such message is relevant here: language is constituted of distinct words, and, however much of a unified story we can tell to bring together all of a word's various uses in a single, articulated meaning, it is hard to resist the suggestion that this meaning is still distinct from that of *another* word—that there are (roughly: synonyms are always possible) as many distinct meanings as there are words. But no such suggestion is in the way when we move from words and language to the seamless medium of thought: there is no reason why the end of the story constituting the meaning of a given word could not be seen as just the end of a chapter in a larger story, connecting the concept expressed by that word to the one expressed by another—and thus making them two phases, two "ideal moments" of *the same* concept.

A genus is itself a particular genus and is essentially related to another, e.g., the idea of the plant to that of the animal; the universal moves on. . . . The genus of the plant has the absolute totality of its realization in the animal, the animal in the conscious existence, just as the earth has it in the plant. This is the system of the whole in which each moment is transitory. . . . Each idea is a circle which is complete in itself, but whose completion is likewise a passing into another circle; it is a vortex whose middle point, that into which it returns, is found directly in the periphery of a higher circle which swallows it up. (*Philosophy* I 346)

Now imagine the limit of this process: a universal story that incorporates all "conceivable" detail, that reaches out to what is expressed by every word, that connects whatever can be thought and talked about. This story is *the* concept—the only one there is.

This simple infinity, or the absolute concept, may be called the simple essence of life, the soul of the world, the universal blood, whose omnipresence is neither disturbed nor interrupted by any difference, but rather is itself every difference, as also their supersession; it pulsates within itself but does not move, inwardly vibrates, yet is at rest. (*Phenomenology* 100)

In the universal concept/story, everything that was alleged to be real ("itself and not another thing") has been turned into an ideal moment (itself *and another*—indeed every other—thing). That there be such a universal structure, that every residue, however recalcitrant, can be conquered by it, is absolute idealism.

The general standpoint of the concept is . . . that of absolute idealism, and philosophy is conceptually comprehensive cognition, insofar as everything which in other forms of consciousness counts as something that is—and because it is immediate, as independent—is known within the concept simply as an ideal moment. (*Logic* 236)[21]

A couple of reformulations of this conclusion are in order, before we continue to voice our worries; for they will help us introduce some important terminology. Something that stands in radical opposition with something else is *limited* by that other thing, and hence, Hegel would say, is *finite*.

To put the point formally, "finite" means whatever comes to an end, what *is*, but ceases to be where it connects with its other, and is thus restricted by it. Hence, the finite subsists in its relation to its other, which is its negation and presents itself as its limit. (*Logic* 66–67)

Correspondingly, something is infinite if it is not limited by anything *else*—if there is nothing to which it stands in radical, irreducible
opposition. It is not a question of size: a very large "infinite" set that
is considered radically distinct from all of its finite subsets would par-
adoxically still count as finite, since those finite subsets would (*only*[22])
be other than it—would not turn out to be (some of) its moments.

> The genuine infinite . . . consists . . . in remaining at home with itself
> in its other. (*Logic* 149)

> The peculiar quality of spirit is . . . to be the true infinite, that is, the
> infinite which does not one-sidedly stand over against the finite but
> contains the finite within itself as a moment. (*Mind* 23)

> The will which has being in and for itself is *truly infinite*, because its
> object is itself, and therefore not something which it sees as *other* or as
> a *limitation;* on the contrary, it has merely returned into itself in its
> object. (*Right* 53)

> If the finite is limited by the infinite and stands on one side, then the
> infinite itself is also something limited; it has its limit in the finite; it
> is what the finite is not, it has something over against it, and it has its
> limit and boundary in that. (*Religion* I 293)

So absolute idealism could also be identified as the thesis that the
concept is infinite—that nothing at all falls outside of it. "[The] ideality of the finite is the most important proposition of philosophy,
and for that reason every genuine philosophy is *idealism*" (*Logic* 152).
"The proposition that the finite is ideal constitutes idealism. The idealism of philosophy consists in nothing else than in recognizing that
the finite has no veritable being" (*Science* 154). "What makes everything *finite* is this and *only* this: that *its being-there is diverse from its
concept*" (*Logic* 99), and every such finite reality is eventually to be
caught in the (infinite) concept's net, indeed "that is what everything
finite is: its own sublation" (*Logic* 128).

This last word "sublation" offers an excuse for another termino-
logical digression. It represents one more awkward attempt to render
the German "Aufhebung" (as "to sublate" does with the cognate verb
"aufheben")—I myself have used less formidable variants like "overcome." This is what Hegel has to say about such words:

> "*To sublate*" has a twofold meaning in the language: on the one hand
> it means to preserve, to maintain, and equally it also means to cause
> to cease, to put an end to. . . . Thus what is sublated is at the same
> time preserved; it has only lost its immediacy but is not on that account

annihilated. The two definitions of "to sublate" which we have given can be quoted as two dictionary *meanings* of this word. But it is certainly remarkable to find that a language has come to use one and the same word for two opposite meanings. It is a delight to speculative thought to find in the language words which have in themselves a speculative meaning; the German language has a number of such. (*Science* 107[23])

So "aufheben" and its cognates are among those words which delight Hegel so much, and that is highly significant because not only are they examples of what he is delighted about: they also account for what it is that he finds delightful. Within Aristotelian, analytic logic—the logic of the understanding—we are stuck with thinking of things as either identical or distinct: "For the understanding, the identical is simply identical, the different simply different" (*Nature* 174). But within the new, dialectical logic Hegel is offering, that very distinction—the distinction between identity and distinctness—can be conquered: one can see the distinct phases of the concept as integral to its complex, articulated unity, as retained within the story that the concept is and at the same time superseded by the later phases of *the same* story. No word says that much in English, and "sublation" is but a technical term in need of a lot of unpacking before it can make any sense at all; so I will continue to stumble along using whatever word feels right at the moment. But yet another version of absolute idealism is suggested by this discussion and by the last indented quote above: everything immediate—everything that just *is*, just presents itself, and because of that stark, ungrounded presence is also set in contrast with everything else that just as ungroundedly is—will have its immediacy eventually sublated: will turn out to be one more vicissitude of the concept, "mediated," and thus perfectly rationalized, by what vicissitudes precede and follow it. Once again, nothing will stay *only* itself: the destiny of all identity is to be *aufgehoben*.

4. Idealism revisited

What Hegel's idealism consists of may be somewhat clearer by now, but that does not mean that its credibility has been established. If anything, this clarification helps identify more precisely what many are going to find absurd in it. For how seriously shall we take the claim that the concept is infinite—that nothing at all opposes it in a radical way? To bring up again an obvious reaction that surfaced before, isn't there a radical opposition between anything conceptual at all—not just the traditional concept *table*, say—and this concrete, material table that I am looking at and knocking on, and trying to make sure I don't knock on too hard or I will hurt myself?[24]

Hegel is fond of using the adjective "concrete" in an approving tone (we have seen one such use on page 30 above), and of contrasting it with the "abstract" concepts we are used to; the distinction "between a conception, a principle, a truth limited to an *abstract* form and its determinate application, and concrete development," he says, "affects the whole fabric of philosophy" (*History* 12). Also, he finds the culmination of the concept in the idea, defined as "*the absolute unity of concept and objectivity*" (*Logic* 286) and hence characterized as what is most properly concrete: "Free and genuine thought is inwardly *concrete;* hence it is *idea,* and in all its universality it is *the* idea or *the absolute*" (*Logic* 38). But what the contrast between abstract and concrete seems to come down to, for him, is how much *richer* the latter is: how far it did not let itself be scared by the prospect of contradiction into withdrawing to some evanescent, unthreatening, uninteresting "core," but rather *used* the contradiction to bring out a more intricate, polyphonic (and yet, importantly, harmonious) version of itself.

> The idea is . . . the *concrete spiritual* unity, whilst the understanding consists in the interpretation of the concept's determinations only in their *abstraction,* that is to say, in their one-sidedness and finitude. (*Logic* 7)

> Everything actual contains opposed determinations within it, and in consequence the cognition and, more exactly, the comprehension of an object amounts precisely to our becoming conscious of it as a concrete unity of opposed determinations. (*Logic* 93)

The sort of thing we are talking about here is, say, the ingenious working out of a true mediation between two political extremes as opposed to a bland, undifferentiated going for "the center," which is equally unappealing to both; the using of a powerful objection to develop one's position as opposed to a precipitous backtracking into some watered-down "common ground"; the painful but profitable learning some truer lesson about oneself from one's "evil past" as opposed to the cowardly blaming of it on external circumstances. And there is nothing wrong with any of that, of course; but it all sounds irremediably "conceptual"—in such a way, that is, as to have no chance of negotiating the chasm between concreteness as detail and concreteness as actual existence.[25]

I will address this fundamental difficulty from both directions, attacking concepts first and then reality. So let's start with concepts. The major obstacle to believing the claim that all there is is a/the concept is that we tend to think of concepts as mental contents—not necessarily as the product of mental activity but in any case as something germane to the mind, something to which the mind, primarily, has access. That, however, is not what Hegel wants us to understand by a concept: "What has usually been called a 'concept' has to be distinguished from the *concept* in the speculative sense" (*Logic* 33).[26]

What, then, is "the concept in the speculative sense"? In answering this question it is helpful to explain, first of all, why, if indeed there is so much difference between concepts as traditionally understood and as understood by Hegel, he continues to use the same word for what he is talking about. Isn't that a regrettable and easily avoidable source of confusion? Hegel himself brings up this issue and handles it as follows:

> Because the concept has a meaning in the speculative logic that is so different from the one that we usually associate with this term, we might raise just the following question: "Why is something that is so completely different nevertheless called 'concept'?" For the result is that an occasion for misunderstanding and confusion is created. The answer to this question must be that, however great the distance between the concept of formal logic and the speculative concept may be, a more careful consideration will still show that the deeper significance of the concept is in no way so alien to general linguistic usage as it might seem to be at first sight. (*Logic* 237)

Part of what is going on here is the general Hegelian strategy of resisting the divisive tendencies of the understanding,[27] since "the true is the whole" and "the whole is nothing other than the essence consummating itself through its development" (*Phenomenology* 11), hence we need "to bring fixed thoughts into a fluid state" (*Phenomenology* 20). I said earlier that distinct words invite one naturally to think of distinct meanings; so if you believe that there is ultimately only one meaning you are going to be very unsympathetic to the common practice of resolving "confusions" by introducing new terms.[28] You will rather want to resolve the confusion into an identity: show how the various senses of one and the same word develop naturally out of one another, how that word's complicated destiny unfolds in a connected narrative. But it is with the questions immediately arising after such a plan is issued that we are concerned here: What exactly *is* the narrative vindicating the unique destiny of this particular word? Why is it, in fact, that the speculative meaning of "concept" is not "so alien to general linguistic usage"?

I have already given the substance of Hegel's answers to these questions when first introducing concepts; I need to extricate the point made there from its context and show its relevance to our current concerns. A concept in the traditional sense is a unifying device, and of course the unity it makes possible is rudimentary, and ultimately a failure: it ends up being the unity of the concept *with itself*, while the things the copula will attach it to are stuck in the uncertain status of irrelevant supplements to it. But still the whole vocation of the concept is expressed in that move—much like the vocation of a future concert pianist is expressed in a three-year-old's awkward fingering those funny white and black keys. What is being expressed is sublation as such: the ideality of the real. This ideality first surfaces around mental stuff and mental occurrences and inclines us to find it natural to say that we can make a foreign object "our own", that we can "appropriate" it without destroying it or even limiting its degree of freedom, by understanding it, by getting to know it. What we need to do now is definitely *not* extend this picture of mentality to the whole world, but rather seize the logical content manifested by the mental and let it develop into something that has nothing necessarily mental about it.

> The concept is the universal which maintains itself in its particulari-
> zations, overreaches itself and its opposite, and so it is also the power
> and activity of canceling again the estrangement in which it gets in-
> volved. (*Aesthetics* 13)

To say that the absolute is the concept is to say that reality is not static, that it is a process, that indeed it must be found precisely in the overcoming of differences which a process *is*. What we tradition-ally understood as concept, or as mind or spirit, brought out that dynamic character in an inchoate form: the concept gathers distinct things; or, this is my world because I represent it to myself, because all those representations are "in me"—whatever any of that means (and it doesn't mean much, Hegel would say: it is still too "abstract"). We need to have the promise intimated by those obscure phrases fulfilled; we need to realize that not just the *res cogitans* is the realm of transmutation and catharsis, but the whole world is. When the promise is fulfilled, we will also realize that the whole world is spirit, which once again does not mean that it looks like the sorts of things we are used to calling spirits, but rather that it is constantly transfiguring itself much as we take spirits—in the limited, "immediate" way in which we have accessed them so far—to be able to do. And realizing that will also amount to finally appreciating the most mature, accomplished sense of the word "concept"—the sense in which concepts are not dead lists of determinate features ("born in the year x, attended school y, published z . . ."), but live, evolving, self-superseding structures.[29]

> Spirit is not an inert being but, on the contrary, absolutely restless being, pure activity, the negating or ideality of every fixed category of the abstractive intellect. (*Mind* 3)

> Spirit's being is . . . only as self-producing, as making itself for itself. . . . Something cannot be perfect from its very beginning, but only when it attains itself, attains its goal. Therefore spirit is this process and is perfect only at its goal. . . . Spirit is essentially this activity of self-production. (*Religion* I 143)

> A conceptual determination, indeed any concept, is not of itself something in repose but something that moves itself; it is essentially activity. (*Religion* II 252)

> The comprehension of the concept of the thing . . . [involves] the concept's development—and hence [the comprehension of] the inner antithesis that the concept contains and through which it moves. (*Religion* III 105)

The outcome of this first line of attack to our problem is deflationary: it seems that we might not be facing as much of a problem as we thought. Hegel's idealism is not the transcendental variety Kant espoused (idealism about concepts *as opposed* to objects): it is a much more robust, metaphysical position. But it is not the kind Kant contemptuously called "empirical," either: there is no Berkeleyan claim in the offing here that reality is constituted of ideas *such as I have in my own mind*. What absolute idealism amounts to, again, is the (metaphysical) claim that what everything is is its history, which is a history of change,[30] a history which will eventually leave nothing (analytically) the same—that there is no analytical essence to be discovered anywhere. And, because everything is forever in the process of turning into everything else,[31] there is in the end only one thing—that we might call conceptual or spiritual simply because such words resonate with the contexts in which we are most likely to be familiar with this kind of phenomenon. Incidentally, "subjective" is also a word we can use to express the dynamic character we are insisting on, because we are also familiar with what we understand empirically as the subject displaying that character more than any object does; thus another way we can express Hegel's position in specifically Hegelian terms is by saying that what there is is not (only) *substance* (meaning by that the inertial structure axiomatized by Spinoza) but (also) *subject*.[32]

> In my view, . . . everything turns on grasping and expressing the true, not only as *substance*, but equally as *subject*. . . . The living substance is being which is in truth *subject*, or, what is the same, is in truth actual only insofar as it is the movement of positing itself, or is the mediation of its self-othering with itself. (*Phenomenology* 9–10)[33]

And yet, this approach does not resolve all our perplexities. A good way of signaling what still remains puzzling about it, and of introducing my second line of attack, is by making more precise what the outcome above actually says. When Hegel claims that being is the concept (or is spirit), he is not just saying that being is dynamic: he is saying that being *is dynamism*.[34] His view is not that there is always change going on, but rather that *there is nothing other than change*: "Truth is its own self-movement" (*Phenomenology* 28). Some (among them, Kant[35]) have argued that, because there is change, we must be able to think of something that is permanent through it; and of course we might eventually convince ourselves (if we are Kant) that this absolutely permanent thing (or matter) is an unrealizable rational ideal. But here the important thing is: Hegel does not share any such conclusion or ideal.[36] There is for him nothing *to which* spiritual movement "happens" (however ineluctably)—spiritual movement is the whole.

> The concept . . . is the simple negative into which all determination, all that is existent and individual sinks. . . . The concept is just the constant change of Heraclitus, the movement, the causticity, which nothing can resist. Thus the concept which finds itself, finds itself as the absolute power before which everything vanishes; and thereby all things, all existence, everything held to be secure, is now made fleeting. (*Philosophy* I 352)

Of course, this is not to say that the movement is always fast, or even noticeable: there will be occasions when it grinds to a halt.[37] Even then, however, we must not think that some "real residue" is finally emerging: the "substance" that moves. Any such substance—

any "material" to which the process "applies"—is but a product of the process itself, a temporary crystallization of it:

> [Spirit] makes war upon itself—consumes its own existence; but in this very destruction it works up that existence into a new form, and each successive phase becomes in its turn a material, working on which it exalts itself to a new grade. (*History* 73)

So we need to focus on reality now—on what we often take reality to be: an inert, self-identical stuff that "goes through" whatever process might occur. And the natural Hegelian site to inhabit as we perform this focusing exercise is one I already alluded to: the section on sense-certainty in the *Phenomenology*. There we are told that any attempt at reaching for the alleged stuff our judgments are supposed to be about is going to end in failure—that indeed precisely the words we take to be most appropriate for such attempts make the failure most painfully obvious.

> It is as a universal too that we *utter* what the sensuous [content] is. What we say is: "this," i.e., the *universal* this; or, "it is," i.e., *being in general*. Of course, we do not *envisage* the universal this or being in general, but we *utter* the universal; in other words, we do not strictly say what in this sense-certainty we *mean* to say. But language, as we see, is the more truthful; in it, we ourselves directly refute what we *mean* to say, and since the universal is the truth [content] of sense-certainty and language expresses this true [content] alone, it is just not possible for us ever to say, or express in words, a sensuous being that we *mean*. (*Phenomenology* 60)[38]

The first thing this passage brings out is controversial but not especially striking: it is the thesis (already mentioned above) that all that can be *said* (in language) is universal. Demonstratives are indeed the most universal of terms. But, if that were all Hegel is claiming, he would be forced into one or the other of the following two positions: either (1) whatever specifically individual things there might be in the world, we cannot talk about them, hence we might as well disregard them, or (2) the world is constituted on the basis of what we can talk about. In neither of those positions would it make much sense for Hegel to claim, as he does here, that language is *truthful*—that, contra the very intentions we might have in using it, it is forcing us to speak the truth.

Hegel does not have a common understanding of "truth" (as indeed he does not of any word—especially philosophically important ones). What he says about it is this:

> In the ordinary way, what we call "truth" is the agreement of an object
> with our representation of it. . . . In the philosophical sense, on the
> contrary, "truth," expressed abstractly and in general, means the agree-
> ment of a content with itself. (*Logic* 60)[39]

Applying this understanding to the previous passage, we get the
following reading of it: whenever we try to refer to a table, or a chair,
or whatever, so as to bring out its radically individual character, what
(allegedly) there is in it that no universal can capture, we are trying
to violate the nature of that thing, to make it incoherent with itself.
Which of course we cannot do, and language shows it and (if we pay
attention) forces us to admit it: we end up being unable to do what
we intended.

So what Hegel is claiming in the *Phenomenology* is not (only) that
language has certain limitations, or that the world is (best) construed
on the basis of language and its limitations: he is (also) saying that
there is a wisdom to language—because those "limitations" are intimations of what the world is like.[40] Once again, his is a metaphysical
thesis—which is once again best understood starting with Kant. In
the Proof of the Thesis of the Second Antinomy (*Critique of Pure
Reason* A434ff B462ff), Kant argues that, if everything were divisible
and "if all composition were annulled in thought, then there would
remain no composite part and (since on this supposition there are no
simple parts) also no simple part; hence there would remain nothing
at all, and consequently no substance would have been given." Either
there are simple parts somewhere, in other words, or everything will
turn out to be made of nothing—and hence *to be* nothing. But this
conclusion depends on conceiving a thing (a substance) as an ultimate
subject of predication—a subject that cannot be turned into a predicate of anything else.[41] It depends, that is, on accepting as an ines-
capable and irreducible constraint of thought the *duality* of subject
and predicate—or, as one could also say, of form and content. And
Hegel rejects that constraint.

> Absolute form has in its own self its content or reality; the concept,
> not being a trivial, empty identity, possesses in its moment of negativity
> or of absolute determining, the differentiated determinations; the con-
> tent is simply and solely these determinations of the absolute form and
> nothing else—a content posited by the absolute form itself and con-
> sequently also adequate to it. For this reason, this form is of quite
> another nature than logical form is ordinarily taken to be. It is already
> *on its own account truth*, since this content is adequate to its form, or
> the reality to its concept. (*Science* 592–93)

There are two major implications of this Hegelian stance. One finally provides an answer to our ever-recurring worry about what reality consists of. Reality is structure (form) all the way down; content is nothing but more articulate form.[42] One can always interrupt the logical analysis of reality and label the outcome a "this"—meaning by that a placeholder for future analysis. But there is nothing definitive about that interruption, and no ultimate subject of predication: the series of determinations is infinite, there is nothing but determinations. The world is a strange attractor, we might say in more fashionable language: every part of it contains an infinity of detail.[43] And, of course, all of these determinations are always developing, turning into one another, contracting and expanding their range—the range of how many *other* determinations they capture. There is no way to keep this butterfly under control.[44]

The second implication has to do with divisions in philosophy. I have characterized some crucial claims of Hegel's as metaphysical; but now it turns out that the very same claims could also be called *logical*. Studying that dynamic character of the world which most immediately surfaces, in our experience, within thought determinations is *the same thing as* studying the world, because that's what the world is: an infinitely dynamic structure—indeed dynamism itself. Hence "*logic* coincides with *metaphysics*" (*Logic* 56), "the science of logic . . . constitutes metaphysics proper" (*Science* 27), "metaphysics . . . is logic" (*Science* 360). "Metaphysics is nothing else but the entire range of the universal determinations of thought, as it were, the diamond net into which everything is brought, and thereby first made intelligible" (*Nature* 11).

The first *Critique* has two major parts (leaving aside prefaces, introduction, and appendix—which is in essence what the Transcendental Doctrine of Method is): the Transcendental Aesthetic and the Transcendental Logic. Given that knowledge for Kant requires both intuition and thought, one would expect those two parts to have equal dignity; but if one looks at their size one realizes that the former is only (in the B pagination) 40 pages and the latter is 660! So, since the first *Critique* covers a lot of the ground traditionally covered by metaphysics and epistemology, there is a very concrete sense in which logic shows a tendency in it to swallow those traditional fields, and what it is to be or to know a tendency to reduce to what it is to reason or to think.[45] Such a tendency culminates in Hegel: logic is now the most universal of disciplines.[46]

At the end of Chapter 1, we were left with the following (Aristotelian) predicament: no portion of science's vocabulary can ever be finally established, logic cannot provide "substantive" research with a repertory of terms of which it is conclusively certain that they have the structure needed for the integrity of that research. Struck by this unwelcome result (and unwilling to tame it by simply making up a new, technical vocabulary), we decided to take a look elsewhere. What emerges now, in the course of taking such a look, is one more instance of how in philosophy problems are not solved but *appreciated*: embedded in a finer, subtler understanding of the human condition.[47] As logic proceeds to take over all substantive disciplines, we begin to realize that in Hegel's perspective the perpetual search for the semantics of terms which logic has turned out to be—the following of semantic development through innumerable twists and turns, beyond countless sublations—coincides with science itself. The ideal of a tool that could be delivered in advance, before any intellectual engagement with any specific content, was challenged by the suggestion that the tool may never be ready for delivery after all; and the response to that challenge, as now becomes clear, has not consisted of making it go away but of embracing it. Yes, indeed: there will never be a time when we can set logic aside and proceed to apply it. Doing dialectical logic is the same thing as "applying" it—if that word even makes sense.

As it turns out, Hegel does claim a finality of sorts for the science of logic—the science *which is* logic. We will have to see what that means, and whether we can be happy with it. And then, before it's all over, we will have to revisit this issue one more time.[48]

THREE

SPIRITUAL MOVEMENT

The ambiguity surrounding my use of the word "story" has already surfaced: On the one hand, a story is supposed to provide whatever content a concept has (and the universal story should supply the content of *the one and only* concept there ultimately is)—which is in principle compatible with such a story being haphazard and messy, and even making no sense at all. On the other hand, the latter is definitely not the kind of story Hegel has in mind; in fact, if the story allegedly telling the truth about the world (history, that is) were to reduce to something like that, he would insist that there is no truth to it.

To put the same point differently, a story allows for surprising incidents, for a character to go through momentous transformations and emerge as a totally novel being—and that fits well with *some* of the things Hegel says about the concept. There is development to it (*Logic* 237); it is a *creative* agency.

> Certainly the concept must be considered as a form, but it is a form that is infinite and creative, one that both encloses the plenitude of all content within itself, and at the same time releases it from itself. (*Logic* 236)

But Hegel also claims that the concept proceeds with absolute necessity—in the terms used here, that the story associated with it is also a demonstration.

The movement [of logic] starts from the first and by correct inferences arrives at the last. (*Science* 71)

[One must] take up the development of the concept, and submit one's thinking, indeed, one's whole heart and mind, to the logical necessity of the concept. (*Logic* 16)

The activity of the concept is to grasp as necessarily determined what to sense-consciousness appears as contingent. (*Nature* 284)

Hegel's concept and the narrative account I have been providing for it are under stress. To perceive the stress more clearly, consider Aristotelian logic again: a word is associated there with a collection of traits, and once the association is made we will be able to infer with necessity that the things referred to by the word have those traits—to extract from the word's semantics what we put there in the first place. All of that is straightforward and provides a sensible account of (some of) what "necessity" means, but what about claiming now that the collection of traits associated with a given word are *necessarily* collected as they are? That, we know, is Aristotle's problem of distinguishing essential from nonessential compounds, and we have seen how much of a problem it is. Analogously, for Hegel, once the semantics of a word (or a concept) is given in terms of a story, all sorts of necessities might be derivable from it, but what sense does it make to say that the story itself proceeds with necessity? It sounds as if the necessity that really does the work here is one that *precedes* semantical assignments; and what could that be?[1]

1. Probability

At *Mind* 278–79, Hegel is attacking a view of history—and specifically the history of philosophy—that invokes impartiality and "demands that the historian shall bring with him no definite aim and view by which he may sort out, state, and criticize events, but shall narrate them exactly in the casual mode he finds them, in their incoherent and unintelligent particularity." And here is how he judges this approach:

A history without such aim and such criticism would be only an imbecile mental divagation, not as good as a fairy tale, for even children expect a *motif* in their stories, a purpose at least dimly surmiseable with which events and actions are put in relation.

This passage forces us once more to bring together "history" and "story." According to the view Hegel antagonizes here (and throughout), the two kinds of enterprise have entirely different standards of success: stories may well have to have a motif (whatever that means), but history need only be true—and there is no reason to think that any motif (or moral) should surface in a succession of true statements about what events have in fact taken place. (Indeed, one might go even farther and claim that a history that sounds too "pat," that makes "too much" sense, is highly suggestive of falsity and deception—possibly *self*-deception.) But Hegel is claiming that, whatever other criteria might also apply to it, history must be at least "as good as" stories are.[2] Fairy tales do not belong to a different line of business from, say, the "tale" of the Roman Empire: they are a much more modest, limited, but still just as genuine outcome of the same activity. So what is required of them must a fortiori be required of "true" history. Whatever else it is, history must also be a good story.

What, then, is a good story? The most elementary condition Hegel would have to set, since we are talking here about the story articulating the one and only concept, is that there be unity to it. And, to see how unity can be achieved, it will be instructive to turn our attention to Aristotle's *Poetics*.

It is not enough for a story to be one, we are told there, that it be the story of one character:

> The unity of a plot does not consist, as some suppose, in its having one man as its subject. An infinity of things befall that one man, some of which it is impossible to reduce to unity; and in like manner there are many actions of one man which cannot be made to form one action. (2322)

That is why there is for Aristotle a substantial difference between the poet and the historian (and an intimate resonance between the poet and the philosopher), since he takes the historian to just report on real events—however confused or even absurd they might be. But we know by now that Hegel rejects that distinction, so let us focus on what the poet is supposed to do.

"The poet's function," Aristotle continues, "is to describe, not the thing that has happened, but a kind of thing that might happen, i.e., what is possible as being probable or necessary" (2322–23). The two words "probable" and "necessary" (or their cognates) regularly occur together in this text: the universal statements that poets (and philosophers, but not historians) are likely to make are those to the effect of "what such or such a kind of man will probably or necessarily say or do" (2323), and a plot is called "episodic" (which is a bad thing to be) "when there is neither probability nor necessity in the sequence of its episodes" (2323).[3] Taking such occurrences at face value might convince us that, according to Aristotle, a good story can contain two kinds of incidents: those which are probable and those which are necessary. But, for that to be an accurate reading, it would have to be the case that good stories can contain necessary developments *that are not probable*. Which is definitely not the case: probability is the controlling notion here, so much so that, if needed, we are to purchase it even at the cost of *impossibility*.

> There should be nothing improbable among the actual incidents. If it be unavoidable, however, it should be outside the tragedy, like the improbabilities in the *Oedipus* of Sophocles. (2327)

> A likely impossibility is always preferable to an unconvincing possibility. The story should never be made up of improbable incidents; there should be nothing of that sort in it. (2337)[4]

So a more accurate understanding of the relation between "probable" and "necessary" here is that the former constitutes *an account of* the latter in the context of storytelling. That is, (a) what makes a story hold together as one is that the incidents comprising it strike the reader (or the audience, in the case of a play) as the sorts of events that would *have to* follow one another, and (b) what *that* means is that they are the sorts of events the reader can recognize as *typically* following one another—since a probability "is a thing that happens for the most part" (*Rhetoric* 2157).

One element of contrast between Aristotle and Hegel is the former's claim that both a narrative and the matter it describes proceed linearly, from a beginning through a middle to an end, and the latter's parallel insistence on circular structures:

> [A] tragedy is an imitation of an action that is complete in itself, as a whole of some magnitude. . . . Now a whole is that which has beginning, middle, and end. A beginning is that which is not itself necessarily after anything else, and which has naturally something else after it; an end is that which is naturally after something itself, either as its necessary or usual consequent, and with nothing else after it; and a middle, that which is by nature after one thing and has also another after it. A well-constructed plot, therefore, cannot either begin or end at any point one likes; beginning and end in it must be of the forms just described. (*Poetics* 2321–22)[5]

The essential requirement for the science of logic is . . . that the whole
of the science be within itself a circle in which the first is also the last
and the last is also the first. (*Science* 71)

Philosophy shows itself as a circle that goes back into itself; it does not
have a beginning in the same sense as the other sciences, so that the
beginning only has a relation to the subject who takes the decision to
philosophize,[6] but not to the science as such. (*Logic* 41)

Suppose we read this contrast literally: we take the classical Bekker
edition of the Aristotelian corpus—which of course has a beginning,
a middle, and an end—and close it in a circle,[7] so that by the time
we get to the *Poetics* we are ready to start all over again with the
Categories and, most important here, to make the experience acquired
through a reading of the whole corpus relevant to a new understanding of the logical treatises—including what sense it makes for something to be (logically) necessary.[8] Then the following suggestion arises:
The necessity with which the Hegelian concept proceeds is narrative
necessity, the one articulated by Aristotle in his description of a good
plot. Each phase of the concept behaves like a character in a well-
connected story: however peculiar the incidents she goes through and
the reactions she has to them, we can recognize her as the same person
throughout because those are the reactions which, on the basis of our
experience, we would expect someone like that to have to similar
solicitations.

So this is how, in general, the ever-recurring Aristotelian worry
that universals might turn out to be just words, and the subject matter
they presume to unify might fall apart, is going to be addressed in the
present context (in specifically Aristotelian terms): What makes the
difference between the *Iliad* and the various (mediocre) *Heracleids* or
Theseids, and establishes "Homer's marvelous superiority" (*Poetics*
2335), is that those other poems were brought together as one *only*
by a proper name, whereas Homer "did not attempt to deal even
with the Trojan war in its entirety" (*Poetics* 2335), and by being more
selective was able to construct "an action with a unity of the kind
we are describing" (Poetics 2322)—the sort of action, that is, whose
various components will appear "probable or necessary." Pace Aristotle, then, the *Iliad can* be a definition, precisely because it is *not* a
"formula whatever" (*Met.* 1626)—as those other, lesser poems were.
There is a single subject matter when there is a single, connected,
"good" story told about it, a story that (by my previous working out
of Hegel's idealism) ultimately turns out to *be* (the same as) its subject

matter, but in any case one that, by relying on what can be expected as likely to happen, vindicates the integrity of a linguistic or conceptual itinerary. In the first *Critique*, Kant refers in passing to this kind of unity:

> In every cognition . . . there is *unity* of the concept; we may call it *qualitative unity*, provided that in [thinking] it we think only the unity in the collating of the manifold of cognitions: e.g., the unity of the topic in a play, a speech, or a story. (B114)

A simple way of expressing my interpretation of the sense of necessity (and unity) that is relevant to dialectical logic is by saying that this marginal remark of Kant's becomes for Hegel the whole ballgame. And what it means for logic to proceed "correctly" from the first to the last, here, is to proceed the way Homer—but not those other, lesser poets—did.[9]

2. Creativity

Earlier it seemed that, though necessity might be a hard thing to assign to a narrative development, the innovative, even revolutionary, character Hegel attributes to the concept's progress might be more at home there. And so it might well be; but still I need to spell out in some detail how creativity and necessity are supposed to go together—how a dialectical turn can be "correct" and surprising at the same time.

Consider a character in a story: Ottilie in the *Elective Affinities*, say, or Karenin in *Anna Karenina*. How does the author handle them? He makes the readers familiar with these people, shows them at work in a number of different circumstances, and so gradually establishes in the readers a sense of what they are like. This sense, importantly, does not reduce to internalizing "if/then" statements concerning such circumstances as those in which the characters have already appeared ("If Eduard shows up, Ottilie feels elated," "If Anna talks to him, Karenin responds in a condescending tone"), but includes counterfactual conditionals whose antecedents have various levels of disconnectedness from those circumstances ("If Eduard made explicit sexual advances to Ottilie, she probably would . . . ," "If Anna became seriously ill, Karenin probably would . . ."). Then, in the "dialectical" moments of the story—the moments of crisis—we find the characters facing extraordinary situations, for which they (and the readers) are not prepared (Ottilie sees Eduard's child drown, Anna tells Karenin that she is Vronsky's lover), and they react in similarly extraordinary ways (Ottilie starves herself to death, Karenin goes through a religious conversion). But, however strange such reactions might be, the read-ers can eventually find them reasonable and still recognize the char-acters *as the same people* (not as having undergone a change of per-sonality—which would make for a very trivial story). Why? Because the seeds for the transformations had already been planted. When they were planted, they were (most likely) not at the center of attention, because the context was different and they were not crucial to it; but still they provided a basis for some of the appropriate counterfactuals, so that now, in the new context, those conditionals can be activated and leave the readers with the reassuring sense that, however uncom-mon the turn of events, the characters had to react to them as they did. Given Ottilie's passive and introspective nature, it makes sense that she would punish herself for the tragedy she has witnessed; given Karenin's arid and conceited shallowness, one can see why, after his comfortable habits have been so dramatically upset, he would fall under the influence of a strong, manipulative person's big words.[10]

In adapting this account to Hegel's case, we have to remind our-selves of the kind of story he wants to tell. Any other story will begin somewhere, with some of its characters already in place and some of what they did already fixed, for reasons that *this* story will not concern itself with. And in any other story there will be an external environ-ment that does not belong to the story line and out of which the changes of context instrumental to the characters' development will often originate. But there is no outside to Hegel's story: what he is telling, we know, is a *universal* narrative. And we also know that there is no beginning or end to it: that it is a circular tale in which every incident both precedes and follows every other incident, and hence both explains it and is explained by it.[11] Therefore, the story must draw all the resources necessary to its unfolding from itself: a "change of context" will only ever be the coming to the fore of something that was already there, a "new character's" entire life must already be written in it, however implicitly, before it ever becomes relevant.

The self-containment Hegel's story must display—or, to put it dif-ferently, the self-sufficiency of the subject matter whose story it is (or, again, because of the idealistic stance, *which* it is)—is highly suggestive of an organism's life. And, indeed, life is for Hegel the immediate idea: the concept that *just* incarnates itself, without providing any explanation, any account of how this is possible. With such qualifications in mind, we can now see clear statements of how creativity is combined with unity and necessity in the concept's "growth" being given by passages like the following:

> Just as in the living organism generally, everything is already contained, in an ideal manner, in the germ and is brought forth by the germ itself, not by an alien power, so too must all the particular forms of living spirit grow out of its concept as from their germ. . . . The concept does not require any external stimulus for its actualization; it embraces the contradiction of simplicity and difference, and therefore its own restless nature impels it to actualize itself, to unfold into actuality the difference which, in the concept itself, is present only in an ideal manner. (*Mind* 5)[12]

Some examples of Hegelian applications of this narrative strategy are in order. So start with the very opening of the story, in the *Science of Logic*: No two concepts seem to be more radically opposed to one another than being and nothing; and yet, when being is characterized as "*pure being*, without any further determination," and as "in its indeterminate immediacy . . . equal only to itself," and nothing as "*pure nothing*," and as "simply equality with itself, complete emptiness, absence of all determination and content," it suddenly strikes us that we are saying exactly the same thing about both, hence that, contrary to what might have seemed, the two coincide. "*Pure being* and *pure nothing* are, therefore, the same" (82). And then we might expect that, if indeed the two coincide, their alleged radical opposition cannot forever mislead us: at some point a structure must come to the fore in which their identity is manifested. This structure is becoming, where being and nothing constantly give way to one another, turn into one another—acting out their essential interchangeability.

Or take a passage a bit later. "The finite . . . ceases to be"; but, as it turns out, ceasing to be is precisely what the finite is. "Thus, in ceasing to be, the finite has not ceased to be; it has become in the first instance only *another* finite which, however, is equally a ceasing-to-be as transition into another finite, and so on to *infinity*" (136). That is, if ceasing to be cannot (only) cancel the finite, the finite must continue inexorably, infinitely to reappear—until some other, more radical resolution for the tension is found. Until, that is, this constant implication of the finite in the infinite, and vice versa, gives way to a more genuine integration of the two.

Or, later still, "resolved contradiction is . . . ground, essence as unity of the positive and negative. . . . Ground is essence as positive identity-with-self, which, however, at the same time relates itself to itself as negativity" (435). That is, if contradiction has asserted itself, then a category must emerge that substantiates it: the category of something which is, and yet whose being is constantly, infinitely referred to another *which is also the same as itself* (thus initiating the dialectic of ground and grounded that will eventually make this category explode).

Or, finally, "effect contains nothing whatever that cause does not contain. Conversely, cause contains nothing which is not in its effect. Cause is cause only insofar as it produces an effect, and cause is nothing but this determination, to have an effect, and effect is nothing but this, to have a cause" (559). So cause and effect will have to bring this intrinsic relatedness to the surface; their destiny, after various frustrating vicissitudes, is to graduate into reciprocal action. "The action, which in finite causality runs on into the spuriously infinite progress, is *bent round* and becomes an action that returns into itself, an infinite *reciprocal action*" (569).

Note two features of these examples: the extension of two familiar narrative techniques to the task of warranting the "correctness" of conceptual connections. On the one hand, a change of context is often created by redescription: we say the same things (what being is, what nothing is, what finitude is) in different words and then hear ourselves speaking, and realize the significance of what we have been saying. It is like dropping a hint in a mystery novel and later making the readers appreciate how much that hint was telling them—how much talking about that person in that way amounted to an indictment of him (Agatha Christie is a master in this technique). On the other hand, the "context" may also be transformed by the inevitable surfacing of something that, once it is proven to exist, cannot be expected to forever stay hidden: someone comes out of the woodwork of whom we know that he was there all along—and had to come out at some point.

The examples make it clear that creativity and necessity coexist in Hegel as distinct points of view on the very same material. When a child "out of the blue" develops an interest for geometry or the flute, or her eyes turn brown, or she asks an important question about the politics of Angola, those witnessing such events will be surprised—and from now on might look at the child differently, think of her as a different person. But in retrospect they might realize that they should have seen it coming, that there was enough in her previous behavior and/or environment to make such turns of events absolutely predictable—if only one had known where to look. So it's not that the child has not become different: she most definitely has. But this difference is the articulation—the very substance, indeed—of a promise that was already implicit in her: the promise of a difference that was formerly *only* implicit and has now come across in full force.

What's tricky here is that Hegel (as usual) wants to have his cake and eat it, too: when we get to the point of *re*cognizing (more about the prefix later) the inevitability of this forward thrust, of this blossoming into view, and become perfectly reconciled with the rationality of it, he also wants us not to forget how creative the move still is, how "explicit" still is something radically richer than "implicit" and cannot be reduced to the latter—how surprise and novelty must be canceled as harmony is reestablished, *but while being preserved*. (The same awkward balancing act was needed with the Aristotelian "potential" and "actual," we know, except that now we can tell more about what unifies the two: narrative connectedness.) So, for him, it is not a matter of oscillating between the different points of view, but of integrating them in a single perspective. Later I will have to say more about how such integration is possible; for the moment, I just notice that by bringing out (usually in different contexts) the different horns of this dilemma, he alleges a perfect "synthesis" of conflict and reassurance.

> Certainly the concept, and furthermore the idea, are self-identical, but they are self-identical only insofar as they at the same time contain distinction within themselves. (*Logic* 181)

> It is . . . the general task of cognition to overcome the contingent. (*Logic* 218)[13]

To take stock of the argument so far, in a language sympathetic to Hegel: (a) The truth of the Aristotelian problem about distinguishing essential from nonessential groupings is that necessity indeed cannot be posterior to a definition, but must be present in the very genesis of it. (b) The attempt to capture this necessity as some kind of intrinsic, *synchronic* relatedness among a variety of traits will forever fall apart in the very *apartness* those traits synchronically show. (c) What is needed instead is a diachronic resolution of their difference in the thematic unity of a development that goes from one to the other, and that is justified by the probability of every step in this development: verity is verisimilitude. (d) Within this approach, all of those limit cases that in the opposite paradigm used to be a source of embarrassment must now be faced in a positive, constructive manner. They

are no longer cases of reality somehow falling short of rational standards—of nature, already "carved at its joints," throwing us off by
building some irrelevant scar tissue. They rather challenge us to continue the story: to show how it is just as necessary to go one additional step beyond any comfort zone we might have reached.

> In a bad plant, a poor specimen of an animal, a contemptible human
> being, a bad state, aspects of its concrete existence are defective or
> entirely obliterated that otherwise might have been adopted for the
> definition as the distinguishing mark and essential determinateness in
> the existence of such a concrete. But for all that, a bad plant or a bad
> animal, etc., still remains a plant or an animal. If, therefore, bad spec-
> imens too are to be covered by the definition, then all the properties
> that we wanted to regard as essential elude us through instances of
> malformations in which those properties are lacking. Thus for example
> the essentiality of the brain for physical man is contradicted by the
> instance of acephalous individuals, the essentiality of the protection of
> life and property for the state, by the instance of despotic states and
> tyrannous governments. . . . The content of definition is in general
> taken from immediate existence, and being an immediate content has
> no justification; the question of its necessity is precluded by its origin;
> in enunciating the concept as a mere immediate, the definition refrains
> from comprehending the concept itself. Hence it represents nothing
> but the form determination of the concept in a given content, without
> the reflection of the concept into itself, that is, *without the concept's being-
> for-self.* (*Science* 799–800)

A comatose patient or a schizophrenic one, or maybe an embryo,
are not to be blamed for failing to comply with our definition of
"human" (which is what treating them as "degenerations" amounts
to); nor are they to be quickly and painlessly included under a new
term that covers both "human" and whatever else they are. The understanding would want to do that, and thereby gain necessity at the
expense of emptiness. But Hegelian reason needs to tell a story instead: an ingenious, cunning, even outrageous story, but also one that
in the end feels just right, to the effect that it is the destiny of "human" to eventually bring coma, or schizophrenia, to the fore.[14]

3. Memory

The probable, I said quoting from Aristotle, is "a thing that happens
for the most part." In traditional storytelling, this clause works in the
following way: as we begin to read a story, we already have an es-

tablished (though perhaps unconscious) sense of what, on the basis of our experience, can be expected to follow from what, and by cleverly playing with those expectations (by cleverly changing the context on us, and hence the generalizations that are relevant to our reading) the author allows us to go through the near-oxymoronic (but still possible, indeed real; which speaks volumes in Hegel's favor) state of discovery—the finding of something *new* that however *was already there*. So, in this ordinary case, probability follows from the (painstakingly worked out) consistency of the story with the larger context of our total experience—with the patterns the latter displays and the habits we have formed as a consequence of repeatedly encountering such patterns.

For Hegel's story, on the other hand, there is no larger context: everything is included in it, so probability cannot issue from consistency with something that holds independently of it. Consistency will still be decisive, but it will be *self*-consistency, *internal* resonance: the patterns relevant to establishing the probability of any individual step will have to be displayed by the story itself, and the habits built on the repeated occurrence of those patterns will have to have been built in the course of acting as a character in that very story. Which, by the way, will impact our understanding of the word "consistency": what is consistent is ordinarily one of many possibilities, but "consistent with our established expectations" already comes close to meaning "deducible from those expectations," and "consistent with a universal story in which everything is connected with everything else" essentially reduces to necessary—and rules out any other option. Hegel would have loved this turning of a meaning into its opposite![15]

The kind of consistency we are talking about is most similar to the overall consistency of a life—*my* life, say, as I gradually reconstruct it on the basis of my memory. Suppose I just did something that at first blush I judged "uncharacteristic" of me: it felt like a foreign object, like the invasion of an alien influence, and it puzzled me—it made me afraid that I was losing control over my actions, that there was no longer any plan expressed in them (certainly not the plan I would have proffered, had I been asked about it before this event happened). So I start reflecting on it and remembering things that were concealed at first: not that I didn't know that they existed, that they were part of me, but I had never brought them together before, I had never thought of them as constituting a pattern—and now I begin to do just that, because of how much I begin to see that they all have something in common (something different in different cases, most likely) with this new, strange thing I observed myself doing. By the end of the process, I may conclude that my formerly perplexing move makes total sense; and if I reach that conclusion then I must also have extracted from my personal archives a different conception of what my "character" is than I was formerly aware of—there must be a different story I am now prepared to tell about who I am. And the resources for this *Aufhebung* have not come from assessing my behavior (what I remember of it) against some external standard, but from assessing it against itself.

In *Religion* III, Hegel gives the following account of philosophy's task:

> The relationship of philosophy [to the truth] is *to grasp conceptually what [already] is*. What is must be *actual* on its own account, before philosophy comes—[it must] not just [be] what is true implicitly, but [must be] in general empirical consciousness. (144)[16]

Since philosophy is the culmination of absolute spirit, the last station of Hegel's journey, and presumably the place where *he* is to be found (and from where he is speaking), we can take this passage as a statement of the task he has been setting for himself. Not all elements of the passage can be accounted for here: specifically, I still have to spell out what the role of consciousness is. But some of it can be made perfectly clear—and help us articulate our current discussion.

Before philosophy goes to work, everything to which it will ever address itself must have already happened—not just in principle, or potentially, but in all actual detail. Philosophy's subject matter is not what will grow tomorrow from seeds planted in the past, but what has already grown, what is already there "on its own account." Philosophy must "grasp conceptually" this "empirical" subject matter: that is, prove that, however confused and confusing it might look on the surface (as is typically the case within the empirical realm), there is a necessary unity to it—which in turn means that it can be told as a convincing narrative. But philosophy is not to venture into what will happen next: it must limit itself to the rationalization of the actual.

On the one hand, this is a project of titanic, even devilish, ambition, that nothing whatsoever is to elude:

> Reason must have confidence in itself, confidence that in nature the concept speaks to the concept and that the veritable form of the concept which lies concealed beneath nature's scattered and infinitely many shapes, will reveal itself to reason. (*Nature* 444–45)

> Reason is the sovereign of the world; . . . the history of the world,
> therefore, presents us with a rational process. This conviction and in-
> tuition is a hypothesis in the domain of history as such. In that of
> philosophy it is no hypothesis. (*History* 9)[17]

But, on the other hand, despite its overweening scope, it is not a
different *kind* of project from the one I attend to when I puzzle over
the many strange incidents of my own history—what of me is actual—and try to understand the logic of it all, the sense it makes, the
"me" that can be told by bringing out some motif from the data I
am facing, by sewing them into the fabric of a single (however ad-
venturous) path. Hegel's logic is one of recollection, of memory, its
necessity is the internal consistency of what is remembered,[18] and in
this sense it is also essentially a phenomenology—*of spirit*, to be sure,[19]
and we are not yet in a position to fully understand what that means,
but still not so distant from the kind of logico/phenomenological
inquiry each of us might occasionally feel inclined, or even urged, to
conduct for her own benefit. For the benefit of one's own sanity, one
will find oneself saying, and then one will reflect that integrity is the
primary component of health, and a *conscious* sense of one's integrity
may be the primary component of spiritual health.

4. Consciousness

I managed to talk about Hegel so far, and even characterize his absolute idealism, with hardly any mention of consciousness. This sits
well with my general view that German idealism has little to do with
its trivial "empirical" counterpart (and just as little with the equally
trivial twentieth-century varieties of phenomenalism). Kant's idealism
is quite different from Hegel's (or, for that matter, from Fichte's or
Schelling's); but they (all) share the thesis that it would be silly to
attempt to reduce "the world" to things going on in our brains, or
minds, or "states of consciousness." This thesis, however, leaves us
with two problems: (a) what, then, qualifies such positions as forms
of *idealism*?, and (b) though consciousness does not have in them the
role it had for Berkeley, it must have *some* (important) role nonetheless, and what could that be?

Leaving Kant (and Fichte, and Schelling) aside here, the answer to
the first question as far as Hegel goes is contained in the analysis
carried out so far: the definitional claim of absolute idealism—that

there are no radical oppositions in reality, and all distinct things will turn out to be distinct phases of the same thing; or, in other words, that reality is an absolutely seamless process—is one with which we are empirically familiar within the range of mental life, the life of ideas and representations. Within the latter, we have a sense (though often only an *immediate*, inarticulate one) that distinct experiences may come together in a single, unitary experience ("experience" in the singular); and indeed that they do so when they "belong with one another," when none of them sticks out as an absurd, incomprehensible exception, when they constitute a coherent whole. What we need to do in order to arrive at absolute idealism is generalize (and articulate) that sense until it covers everything there is—and calling such a generalization "idealism" brings out *the truth of* our previous empirical familiarity. We were on to something exactly right when we felt the way we did about mental life, except that we didn't know *how* right we were—how far the scope of what we felt extended. So we should definitely *not* use a new word for the view we have now developed (as the understanding would like us to): just as we did when we let the infant concept of the tradition grow into the full-fledged dialectical concept, with "idealism" too we should rather do justice to our original intuition in a way that shows what mature state it was promising to develop into.

That part is easy by now; but the second question will require a more elaborate answer. To begin with, note that in the *Phenomenology* Hegel talks about (his) idealism as follows:

> Reason is the certainty of consciousness that it is all reality; thus does idealism express its concept. (140)

And in the same work spirit—which we don't know much about yet, but we do know must be what everything is—receives this characterization:

> Reason is spirit when its certainty of being all reality has been raised to truth, and it is conscious of itself as its own world, and of the world as itself. (263)

That is, reason is consciousness's ungrounded but irresistible inclination to rely on the identity between itself and the "outside" world (a typical example being the scientist, who unreflectively takes "rational" conclusions reached in his own mind to apply to what is not mind); and spirit is consciousness that has become aware of relying on that identity and has found it to be justified.[20] But, then, it definitely seems that consciousness is enormously important in Hegel's scheme of things—indeed, it might even seem that my reconstruction of his idealism is sanitized to the point of inaccuracy.

My response to this challenge comes in two parts: in the remainder of this section I will explain where consciousness comes in, and in the next section I will show what vicissitudes it must go through to emerge as spirit—which will also help further specify how the word "consciousness" is to be understood.

In *Religion* III, Hegel says:

> Consciousness is that there is an object that is simply determined as an other and remains over against me, e.g., a mountain, sun, sky. (166)[21]

So consciousness is the very establishing of a contrast between a subject and an object, of a duality between something that is and a point of view on it; and there is consciousness wherever such contrast, such duality are active—however hidden *that* might be.

In Aristotelian logic, necessity can be thought of as a perfectly objective quality: a quality, that is, which resides entirely in the object. If all those things which are roses are flowers, and all those things which are flowers have petals, then necessarily all those things which are roses have petals—and this fact holds independently of any reference to a becoming conscious of it. It might take great skill and learning to hit upon the right ways of talking about things—those bringing out the necessary connections among them—but such necessary connections are there and do not in any way invoke the participation of a talking or thinking about them.

Hegelian necessity, on the other hand, is to be fleshed out as the connectedness of a good story, and that in turn as the quality which a story has when one can convince oneself that the events constituting it are "probable." But that means that this necessity contains as an essential parameter the presence of a witness to itself, that its articulation demands the establishing of a two-level structure, where one level is *for* the other (to contemplate, to judge the probability of . . .).[22] What Hegel would call consciousness is embedded in it.

Since the point is a delicate one, I will rephrase it a couple of times. It is empirically true that stories (good or otherwise) are read (at least by their authors), and that they are written for the purpose of being read. But that empirical fact will not justify the logical conclusion we are after. It is perfectly possible to think of a "story" that is "written" by the wind on the desert sand, or that comes together in my hard drive by a totally random interaction of electrons;

and it is possible to think of criteria for when a story counts as "good" that are as objective as Aristotelian necessities. We might say that a story is good if it contains exactly twenty-seven chapters, or if every paragraph in it begins with an article, or if all of the words occurring in it also occur (with that precise spelling) in the English dictionary—which of course could also be given a conceptual characterization involving no essential reference to consciousness. But such are not the criteria I have been mobilizing here. What I have said is that a story is good if its incidents cohere with a certain set of expectations, formed on the basis of a certain experience; and it is not possible to understand any of that without bringing in an agency which, on the basis of the experience it had and the expectations it formed as a result, stands in a specific relation to the story. That necessity involves consciousness here has nothing to do with empirical facts about stories: it follows from a simple working out of what necessity has come to *mean* for us. It is, Kant would say, a transcendental matter.

My other reformulation begins by asking a simple, but instructive, question: is it implied by what I said so far that there is always a reader for the Hegelian story, something mind-like that observes its unfolding—just as Berkeley thought that, because *esse est percipi*, God must be constantly charged with the tedious task of keeping everything in existence by perceiving it? Not at all. Because this story is the universal one—indeed, is the universe—there will be large portions of it where consciousness has no role whatsoever: long stretches in which all there is is, say, particles falling in the void and thereby constituting (inanimate) heavenly bodies. But what it means for those portions to have proceeded with necessity—for those particles to have fallen, and constituted heavenly bodies, according to inexorable laws—will only surface in an explicit form when the witness parameter is finally activated, and by reference to it "one" can cash out retrospectively what "falling according to inexorable laws" amounted to. Then "one" will also be able to appreciate how the goodness of the story was already implicit in it (was "in [the story] itself"[23]) before there was any witness; but once again such appreciation would be incomprehensible if it didn't refer to a (later) stage in which the witness is there—just as a shapeless pile of bricks can only be seen as "an incomplete house" by referring to something complete it is in the process of becoming. The story's internal coherence, in other words, must be eventually *re*cognized, without however being *cognized* at all times.

5. Spirit

It is not just any (good) story we are talking about here: it is *the* story of the one and only thing there is—the thing that so far we have mostly been calling "concept" but are now ready to officially give the more appropriate name of "spirit." What is the difference between the two terms? Turn to *Religion* III once more:

> The concept—yes, even the concept—is itself still one-sided when taken as merely implicit; that is how it is in this one-sided form. . . . That is to say, subjectivity is pure knowledge of itself, but a knowledge that is, on its own account, contentless, void of content. . . . What has no objectivity has no content. (168)[24]

The universal story begins by showing that all the major categories of traditional philosophy *necessarily* (in the sense I have described) lead into one another, and hence are all phases of one and the same "thought-determination." But that is not where it ends: what happens next is that this single thought-determination (which means: this single fluid, "ideal" thing) *must* (always in the same sense of this modality) go out of itself, wander into things that are not fluid but rather *external* to one another, into externality as such, into nature.[25] And then gradually "it" must appear that this externality is itself only a phase of the very same thing—that this "error" (in the etymological sense of *errare*) is exactly what was needed for that thing to find its way.[26] "It" must appear to whom? To the story's witness, of course—except that, again, this is the universal story, and the story of only one thing. So that witness must also be the one and only character in the story: it must be *its own* story that it is witnessing. When this becomes clear, spirit has emerged[27]—which of course is not to say that something radically different has emerged, that spirit *is not* (the same as) the concept, but it does mean that we might want to use this different word for the new shape the concept has taken.

> Spirit has resulted as the idea entered on possession of itself. Here the subject and object of the idea are one—either is the intelligent unity, the concept. This identity is *absolute negativity*—for whereas in nature the intelligent unity has its objectivity perfect but externalized, this self-externalization has been nullified and the unity in that way been made one and the same with itself. Thus at the same time it *is* this identity only so far as it is a return out of nature. (*Mind* 8)

> The concept that has determined itself, that has made itself into its own object, has thereby posited finitude in itself, but posited *itself* as

the content of this finitude and in so doing sublated it—that is spirit. (*Religion* III 270)

If consciousness is otherness as such—the distinction of a subject and an object—spirit is the reconciliation of that otherness: the absolute resolution of consciousness into self-consciousness, of otherness into the articulation of unity.

I noted before that it is not enough for a story to be one that it be the story of one character. And it is also the case that many a good story cannot be judged the story of a single person; even in a case as apparently clear as the *Odyssey*, say, we might wonder whether that is the story of Odysseus after all—and not perhaps of Telemachos, or of the two of them. But, though this is neither a necessary nor a sufficient feature of good stories, it is a possible one; and Hegel's story has such a feature, to an extreme. It is time to draw some startling conclusions from this fact, with which we have been living unreflectively for a while—to recognize what they were trying to tell us all along.

Spirit is the one character here. But spirit is the whole thing, the whole world; more precisely, a conceptually very elaborate and perspicuous form the whole world has taken. And this character, insofar as it *is* spirit, is supposed to be conscious of itself, and of the fact that what is being told (by itself) is its own story.[28] Now suppose that the elaborate and perspicuous form we are talking about is a certain political structure, or religious community, or philosophical system—all of these are concrete suggestions one can derive from Hegel. Then what we are saying (among other things) is that this political structure, or religious community, or whatever, *is self-conscious*. And here we get into hazardous terrain: however credible people might have found Hegel so far, most are going to think of such a conclusion as the kind of mystical nonsense they definitely want to steer clear of.

The reason for this sentiment is that one is naturally inclined to run together two distinct matters (as was previously the case with concepts and idealism): the logical structure we have decided to identify as consciousness (or, for that matter, *self*-consciousness) and the empirical manifestations of that structure that we are familiar with. (One is *naturally* inclined to do that, by the way, because that is what the *natural* point of view consists of: seeing the essence of a logical structure in [some of] its external manifestations.) Such manifestations inevitably have a mental quality to them: they consist of the sorts of experiences a (conscious) human would have. So, by running together these two distinct levels of discourse, one is led to believe that, if indeed spirit is the whole world—or, even better, the whole world-history—then there must be a world (or world-historical) *mind*, which works much as our minds do except for having universal scope. And, after reaching that conclusion, one is likely to want to part ways with Hegel.

But the conclusion is unwarranted. Consciousness, again, is nothing but the contrast between a subject and an object, and all that is necessary for two contrasted elements to be qualified as a subject and an object is that one be in some sense "about" the other. Self-consciousness then is nothing but reflexivity, being about oneself, folding over oneself in such a way that one duplicates oneself and at the same time puts forth the identity of the two sides of this duplicating operation. For self-consciousness to apply through a diachronic structure—a narrative, in the terms I have been using here—it has to apply across memory; but once again there is no reason to think of memory as necessarily constituted of mental representations. There will have to be some kind of record, of course, some strategy for making the past present and relevant again, and the folding operation will have to apply to such presentified material. But none of that will have to happen within anything remotely similar to a human mind, and bring about anything similar to the empirical outcome generated when a human mind is indeed in question.

Human minds and experiences occupy a middle position in the development of these logical structures. At one extreme we find them implicit in primitive, brutal forms of life—say, a hungry animal's preying behavior, or even more specifically its starting on a path that has often in the past been conducive to successful preying.[29] It will be only later in the story, when human consciousness surfaces, that the significance of those animal moves will become transparent—only then will they be recognized as intimations of consciousness. But (a) human consciousness will recognize them precisely as earlier phases *of itself*, and (b) it is only because their structure resonates with the structure of human consciousness, because the same spirit animates them, that they can be *recognized* at all. Once again, this is a case of identity in difference—with the emphasis on "identity."[30]

Turn now to the opposite extreme: to what happens in the universal story *after* the surfacing of human consciousness (and memory). And, to begin with, consider a few quotes:

The state is the *self-conscious* ethical substance. (*Mind* 263)

The state is to attain existence as the *self-knowing* ethical actuality of spirit. (*Right* 301)

The state is the spirit which is present in the world and which *consciously* realizes itself therein. . . . Only when it is present in consciousness, knowing itself as an existent object, is it the state. (*Right* 279)

In opposition to the principle of the individual will, we should remember the fundamental concept according to which the objective will is rational in itself, i.e. in its *concept*, whether or not it is recognized by individuals and willed by them at their discretion. (*Right* 277)

The spirit . . . knows and wills itself as having *passed through the form of education*. The state therefore *knows* what it wills, and knows it in its *universality* as something *thought*. (*Right* 290–91)

The Greeks were still unacquainted with the abstract right of our modern states, that isolates the individual, allows of his acting as such, and yet, as an invisible spirit, holds all its parts together. This is done in such a way, however, that in no one is there properly speaking either the consciousness of, or the activity for the whole; but because the individual is really held to be a person, and all his concern is the protection of his individuality, he works for the whole without knowing how. (*Philosophy* II 209)[31]

The following points seem to be clearly stated in these passages: (a) the state is conscious of itself, (b) that the state is conscious of itself is compatible with there being no individual members of it who are conscious (of themselves or of the state) in quite the same way, (c) what it means for the state to be conscious of itself includes that there exists an educational *institution* through which the state maintains contact with its structure and preserves it through time. And, on the basis of (a)–(c), I make the following suggestion: the self-consciousness of the state has nothing mental about it, if by "mental" we understand the sorts of occurrences and qualities that are relevant to *our own* minds.[32] What self-consciousness amounts to, in the state's case, is the existence of reflective practices, such as, but not limited to, educational ones. Parades displaying the state's military strength would be practices of this kind, and so would statements of principle by the legislature, or sentences by the Supreme Court—and they would be that *even if* all individual (human) participants in a parade, all members of the legislature or of the Supreme Court, were personally motivated to play whatever role they play in this affair by greed, inertia, or fear, *and* even if all such participants or members were thoroughly uninterested and bored through the whole event, and totally lacking in any understanding of its significance.[33] The state's memory will be conceived in the same way: as objectively constituted of records, libraries, and documents—being it even clearer in this case that none of it can be reduced to the experiences of any individual human, or even of the collection of all of them. And the state's consciousness of its own memory will consist of various practices that reflect on such records—publications by the librarian of Congress, say, *whatever* the intellectual qualities of the *individual* occupying that position might be.

To move from political to religious language,[34] consider the following:

> This aspect of community is the distinctive region of spirit. The Holy Spirit has been poured out upon the disciples. From then on they exist as a community—the community is their immanent life. (*Religion* III 142)

> The community consists in . . . faith being available for everyone as a presupposition—that is how spirit is universally present. The opposite view is that all of us possess our own doctrine for ourselves; but this is a mere matter of chance, and in religion this privacy of belief is consumed. (*Religion* III 373)

Members of a religious community incarnate spirit insofar as they exist collectively *as a community*; and that community's self-consciousness consists of its immanent practices—its various ceremonies, for example. In this case, too, the extent to which the individual believers consciously appreciate the significance of (say) attending mass is irrelevant to whether or not mass is one such mode of *communal* self-consciousness: what is relevant includes, rather, the specific acts (readings, gestures, touchings) that constitute the fabric of the mass, and that show precisely the same aboutness with respect to the community's values, doctrines, and history that my mental experiences may have with respect to similar elements of my own identity. The scale, of course, is larger, indeed it is tendentially universal—which is what makes this a more adequate manifestation of spirit.

An important qualification must be added to the above, whose meaning will become clearer in Chapter 4. State or religious practices per se, according to Hegel, cannot account for the concept's moment of individuality; and yet that moment is needed, too. That the state (say) is conscious of itself may well entail that there be parades and statements of principle and sentences of the Supreme Court—that there be such institutions, that is. But no single parade or statement of principle or sentence of the Supreme Court would be regarded by Hegel as a case of *individual* self-consciousness. For the latter to be present, the significance of those institutions has to show up to *humans*, however occasionally and imperfectly[35]—though, when that happens (as we will see in Chapter 4), part of what shows up is precisely the identity between each of the relevant individual human self-consciousnesses and the universal moment of the state (or whatever). One might think that imposing this condition amounts (again!) to confusing the logical moment of individuality with the empirical structures (human beings) in which such a moment tends to manifest itself for us—and I would be sympathetic to this criticism. But appreciating the individuality of (physical or virtual) *Übermenschen* may have been one or two *Aufhebungen* away from Hegel. And, in any case, returning to the issue with which we are currently concerned, this condition about individuality, however questionable it might be in itself, has nothing to do with what *the state's own* (universal) self-consciousness is and will definitely not force us to understand *that* in terms of anything like a universal (human-like) mind.

FOUR

THE END OF HISTORY?

Hegel's treatises and lecture series usually end with a strong suggestion of finality: spirit has come to its last station, we are told, and some kind of absoluteness has been achieved. Here are a few representative quotes:

> This last shape of spirit—the spirit which at the same time gives its complete and true content the form of the self and thereby realizes its concept as remaining in its concept in this realization—this is absolute knowing; it is spirit that knows itself in the shape of spirit, or a *comprehensive knowing*. (*Phenomenology* 485) In this knowing, . . . spirit has concluded the movement in which it has shaped itself, insofar as this shaping was burdened with the difference of consciousness, a difference now overcome. Spirit has won the pure element of its existence, the concept. (*Phenomenology* 490)

> The absolute idea . . . [is] the rational concept that in its reality meets only with itself. . . . All else is error, confusion, opinion, endeavor, caprice and transitoriness; the absolute idea alone is *being*, imperishable *life, self-knowing truth*, and is *all truth*. It is the sole subject matter and content of philosophy. Since it contains *all* determinatenesses within it, and its essential nature is to return to itself through its self-determination or particularization, it has various shapes, and the business of philosophy is to cognize it in these. (*Science* 824)

> The eternal idea, in full fruition of its essence, eternally sets itself to work, engenders and enjoys itself as absolute spirit. (*Mind* 315)

66

It is hard to come away from passages like these without feeling that Hegel considers himself and his philosophy as the culmination of world history: that, according to him, "from now on" (if that expression even makes sense) nothing is supposed to "happen" (with the same qualification) other than the eternal spinning out of some universal and infinitely articulate structure. And this (alleged) view of his has given rise to all sorts of charges and ironies, stigmatizing its (apparent) absurd arrogance, complacent optimism, and sheer gullibility. We can get no clear sense of what role Hegel might play on the contemporary scene without taking a position on the various issues surrounding these claims and accusations—which I intend to do in the present chapter.

1. Rational comprehension

My first move on this terrain is a deflationary one, intended to show that there is not as much of a problem here as some think. Eventually, I will argue that the problem is not smaller (or greater) but *different* than is often taken to be. However, in order to get to that stage, I need to explode the worries that tend to monopolize the (bad) press.

My starting point is a famous text from the preface to the *Philosophy of Right*:

> This treatise, . . . insofar as it deals with political science, shall be nothing other than an attempt *to comprehend and portray the state as an inherently rational entity.* As a philosophical composition, it must distance itself as far as possible from the obligation to construct a *state as it ought to be;* such instruction as it may contain cannot be aimed at instructing the state on how it ought to be, but rather at showing how the state, as the ethical universe, should be recognized. . . . To comprehend *what is* is the task of philosophy, for *what is* is reason. As far as the individual is concerned, each individual is in any case a *child of his time;* thus philosophy, too, is *its own time comprehended in thoughts.* It is just as foolish to imagine that any philosophy can transcend its contemporary world as that an individual can overleap his own time or leap over Rhodes. If his theory does indeed transcend his own time, if it builds itself a world *as it ought to be,* then it certainly has an existence, but only within his opinions—a pliant medium in which the imagination can construct anything it pleases. (21–22)[1]

Two major things are to be found in this passage: a clear statement on Hegel's part of what his intellectual project is, and some disparaging remarks directed at all those involved in projects of a different nature. Given the polemical tone of the latter, more attention is likely to be focused there; but in fact the criticisms are vain, since they reduce (as we will see) to pointing out that those other projects fail to meet the criteria appropriate *to Hegel's*—a case of "mak[ing] use of . . . [one's] own bright ideas and thoughts during the course of the inquiry" (*Phenomenology* 54) if there ever was one. It is still the case that choosing one project as opposed to others is an operation of enormous intellectual and social significance; hence later I will have to bring up and discuss that choice. But for the moment we need to concentrate on what exactly Hegel's project amounts to.

Return to the task of making sense of my individual life. If successful, it issues in reconciliation and contentment: despite the original intimations of trouble, my house is in order after all—my biography can be read as a good story. Now consider two distinct objections that could be raised against such self-satisfied conclusion. On the one hand, it might be pointed out to me that I forgot an important detail, and one that, when looked at, shows a perplexing inclination to throw off my hard-won consistency; on the other hand, I might be reminded that, however harmonious an identity I have attained, it is unlikely that the next incidents in which I take part will fit too easily with it—indeed, it would not be so good if they did, for then my life would have nothing more to tell me.

> It would be desperately wearisome to have exact foreknowledge of one's destiny and then to live through it in each and every detail in turn. (*Mind* 112²)

The first objection would disturb me, because (if correct) it would prove that I failed at the specific task I was setting for myself; and I would feel urged to go back to the drawing board and try to find a (coherent, harmonious) place for the forgotten detail. But my reaction to the second objection would just be to shrug my shoulders: *of course* I know that, I would say, but it is irrelevant—living new incidents is one thing, and rationalizing them is quite another. Setting my house in order is not something I will only do once; but thinking now, *as* I am doing it, that I will have to do it again can only be a lazy distraction from the obligation (or the destiny) I might have (as a rational being) of doing a good job of it *now*. Think of a slob who never dusts his shelves because inevitably dust will cover them again, and you will know what I mean.[3]

What the example brings out is that there are two senses in which a Hegelian story could make a claim to being comprehensive—indeed to being the ultimate story. The first sense is that all chronology has been redeemed: everything that is, and was, the case has been proved necessary. The second is that no other story of the same kind will ever be told: the world (that is, spirit) is at an end. But the latter not only is not—it *cannot* be what Hegel means. Spirit is infinitely creative: for it to reach its final destination is also for it to die, and spirit cannot die—or, better, even its occasional death is part of its life.[4] Spirit will continue to grow beyond whatever story Hegel (or anyone) tells; and it will continue to do so in ways no story *now* can fathom. For, again, if any story could predict the future course of spirit, the latter's creativity would be exhausted and its "life" would lose all significance.

So it is the first sense that is relevant here: one must make sure that, in the words already quoted once,[5] "*what [already] is*, . . . [what is] *actual* on its own account, before philosophy comes" is given due consideration—that consistency is not gained at the expense of concreteness,[6] by separating out a thin layer of rationality from an inarticulate, disorderly mess ("I am not *that*: that just happened to me, and I cannot be identified with it, nor can one get any sense from it of what I am like"). The best evidence of Hegel's extreme sensitivity to this issue is his practice: his relentless exploration of *all* subject matters, his constant incorporation into new editions of his lectures of all the data he could lay his hands on, and his sustained attempt at making sense of every bit of such data, at leaving none of it unresolved. It is the sort of attitude for which he has often been chastised and ridiculed—the one involved in his "proving" (say) that Greek sculpture could not have adopted "material unnecessary for the specific stage at which it [stood]" and hence could not have "avail[ed] itself . . . of a painter's colors but only of the spatial forms of the human body" (*Aesthetics* 706), when in fact those sculptures, at the stage at which they stood, were mostly colored (and Hegel was simply misinformed about it). And, of course, from a different point of view this very attitude might be seen as heroic and the object of admiration. But for us now it is less important to decide among such conflicting value judgments than to understand the attitude itself: what its objective is, and how the nature of that objective determines what the standards for success are—in particular, (a) what sorts of factors will be regarded as evidence of failure and (b) what others will be judged orthogonal, hence indifferent, to the activity at hand.

I will have more to say later about (a); specifically, about some important qualifications that must be made to (a naive understanding of) it. Right now, I am interested in (b), since fleshing it out will give us the deflationary conclusion I am looking for. That Hegel is at the end of history is not an ambitious metaphysical claim about the structure of history, but an immanent feature of Hegel's philosophical stance—as much a conceptual requirement for it as we saw reference to a consciousness to be. Everyone is at the end of (her own) history when she takes the retrospective, rationalizing position with respect to it Hegel is taking; everything has already happened for her because, trivially, the range of that "everything" is precisely what has already happened.[7] The demands she will put on herself within that range are extreme: either the whole thing can be made to work or the whole thing is bankrupt. But there are no other demands: no reference to other, possible, future data even makes sense. Another day we will play another game—but even *that* statement has no currency in the game we *are* playing. And at times Hegel says just that, which is how I read his criticism of the alternative in the passage from the *Philosophy of Right* set off above (and why I think of that criticism as circular—a case of just reasserting his position): there are people who think that they can direct the future course of politics toward some desirable end, but they are deluded, *because such utopian recommendations can never present themselves, by their very nature, as having the same kind of logical inevitability a "rationally comprehended" past has.*

One last twist must be added before I move to a related topic, and that has to do with where exactly Hegel is situated with respect to the data he is considering. I played fast and loose above with the distinction between past and present—because then I intended to contrast both with the future. But the past and the present *are* distinct, and we must now face up to that issue. Hegel wants to understand *his own* time, the time in which he is living, the one that is contemporaneous with him. He also says, however, that the only data relevant to his rationalizing task concerns what has *already* happened. The conjunction of these two statements leaves one with the strange conclusion that Hegel would have to be seeing his own present as past— that in some way he would have to have a *future* position with respect to it. This strange conclusion is exactly right, and to begin to substantiate it I turn to a passage from Sartre's *Psychology of Imagination*:

> This is what happens when our eyes wander over wall paper when we lie inactive during an illness. It then happens that a familiar form springs up from these arabesques, that is, a somewhat coherent synthesis is formed in the course of these movements under my gaze: my eyes have traced a path which remains traced on the tapestry. Then I say: it is a man in a squatting position, it is a bouquet, a dog. That is, I construct a hypothesis on this spontaneously operated synthesis: I at-

tribute a representative value to the oriented form that had just appeared to me. Most of the time I do not even wait for this synthesis to complete itself, but suddenly something crystallizes into something that is about to become an image. "This is beginning to look like a bouquet, or the upper part of a face, etc." (47)

This passage holds the secret of the complex relationship between Hegel's rational reconstruction and his time. His is not *only* a reconstruction of the empirical past—of what, *as a matter of fact*, is past—and is certainly not a sketch of a utopian (nowhere-to-be-found) future: it is the tracing of an *imminent* future, one whose current (empirical) nonexistence is logically irrelevant, because all of its pieces are already in place and its pattern is already emerging. Hegel is located at the threshold of the future: after everything there is but before everything there isn't (yet)—in a sort of future perfect in which the auxiliary "I will" always applies to a content perceived as past. And, as it turns out, there is a specifically Hegelian way to say that:

> It is a present that raises itself, it is essentially reconciled, brought to consummation through the negation of its immediacy, consummated in universality, but in a consummation that is not yet achieved, and which must therefore be grasped as *future*—a now of the present that has consummation before its eyes; but because the community is posited now in the order of time, the consummation is distinguished from this "now" and is posited as future. (*Religion* III 188)[8]

Two important consequences follow from this temporal topology. First, it is consistent for Hegel to refuse utopian thinking while at the same time exposing the limitations of current society (or religion, or art, or whatever—which he often does[9]) *and* while seeing and describing the present as bustling with activity and innovation, while saying things like "ours is a birth-time and a period of transition to a new era" (*Phenomenology* 6). His point of view is much like Moses': he sees the promised land before anyone else does. But that promise is a reflection from his understanding of the past *and of the present perceived as past*—hence is always based on what is *logically* past.

Second, it is also clear now why there can be Hegelian "projects" but there cannot be any significant amount of detail to them: they cannot tell any articulate story about what in fact will happen. Take the Hegelian story told by Marx: it frustratingly stops right at the moment when one would want to know more—to get specific information about the structure society will have after capitalism's collapse and the proletariat's triumph. We are now able to see that the reason for this frustration is transcendental, not empirical: that it is not the sort of frustration we would feel if one did a bad job of typing a paper, but the sort we would feel if we expected someone to type using a pocketknife—in general, if we expected some outcome to be delivered by the wrong tool. Like Hegel, Marx sits in the imminent future, in the place where the patterns governing our present suddenly show up (as in Sartre's example), and that abrupt, instantaneous— hence also simple, unstructured—crystallizing experience is all that he is asking of the future and all the role it can play for him. There is no dimension, no thickness to it, nor is there any independent intellectual dignity: "the future" is only a terrace (a very narrow one—like those in Siena's Piazza del Campo) from which to look at all that is.

2. Contingency

I suggested before that qualifications must be added to (a naive un- derstanding of) the radical claims Hegel often makes concerning the standards of his rationalizing activity. That "development by means of the concept . . . [admit] of no contingency" (*Religion* I 167) or that it be "the general task of cognition to overcome the contingent" (*Logic* 218) is compatible with contingency still being present, and playing a major role, in his view.[10] Three such roles, as a matter of fact— which I now need to bring out.

The first role reminds us of the second-order consistency (or prob- ability) Aristotle thought compatible with first-order inconsistency (or improbability).[11] Just as some characters are consistently inconsistent (and just as it is probable that some improbable things will happen), it is not a contingent matter (it is necessary) that there be contingent matters. Contingency is a definite feature of reality, and like every other feature it is telling us something; typically, it is voicing the externality into which the concept must wander before finding itself again and finally emerging as spirit.

> In common life all is real, but there is a difference between the phe- nomenal world and reality. The real has also an external existence, which displays arbitrariness and contingency, like a tree, a house, a plant, which in nature come into existence. (*Philosophy* II 95)

> Nature just signifies the lack of power to be perfectly adequate to the concept; it is only in spirit that the concept has its true existence. (*Philosophy* III 309)

So it is perfectly appropriate that there be stages in our narrative
in which a bunch of things simply are or occur, with no rhyme or
reason.[12]

> Nature in its manifestations does not hold fast to the concept. Its wealth
> of forms is an absence of definiteness and the play of contingency; the
> concept is not to be based on them, rather it is they which are to be
> measured by the concept. (*Nature* 299)

> The concept ... exerts its influence ... only to a certain degree. ...
> One must not ... seek conceptual determinations everywhere, al-
> though traces of them are everywhere present. (*Nature* 418)

And one must avoid being led astray by such contingency: miss
the forest for the trees, fail to perceive that all of this noise, all of this
error and confusion are necessary concomitants of the inevitable triumph of rationality:

> In affirming ... that the universal reason *does* realize itself, we have
> indeed nothing to do with the individual empirically regarded. That
> admits of degrees of better and worse, since here chance and speciality
> have received authority from the idea to exercise their monstrous
> power. Much, therefore, in particular aspects of the grand phenomenon
> might be found fault with. ... The insight then to which ... philos-
> ophy is to lead us, is, that the real world is as it ought to be—that the
> truly good—the universal divine reason—is not a mere abstraction, but
> a vital principle capable of realizing itself. (*History* 35–36)

The second sense in which contingency has a place here can be
gathered by accounting for what it means that "traces of ... [con-
ceptual determinations] are everywhere present." Understanding a
natural occurrence as a *trace* of a conceptual determination requires
adopting a retrospective attitude toward it: seeing it as the sort of
thing that, in the subtler, deeper language appropriate to a later phase
of the narrative, could be described as expressive of a conceptual
determination. But, of course, there is also a language appropriate to
the very phase of the narrative where the natural occurrence occurs,
and in that language the conceptual determination will probably find
no expression, hence neither will the necessity that accompanies the
concept—and trying to cook up some "extrinsic" necessity within
such an unsophisticated language would only generate absurdities.
Thus, for example, one can see in retrospect why the simultaneous
attraction and repulsion particles exercise on one another in the void
is a necessary (albeit rudimentary) expression of their identity *and*

difference, but it would be a mistake to try to establish the necessity of those forces within the vocabulary of (Newtonian) particle physics: in that language, they are to be taken as simply *being there*.[13]

What complicates matters is that, according to Hegel, nothing is *just* a mistake. Take phrenology, which is a good example of what I am talking about: the "science" that claimed to discover people's character and inclinations by studying the conformation of their skull.[14] Hegel gives it as good a thrashing as I have seen him give anything—those who practice it, he suggests, should not just receive a box on the ear, but have their skull beaten in, so as to make it very vivid to them what the nature of a bone is. And yet, though even "the crude instinct of self-conscious reason will reject [it] out of hand," phrenology teaches us an important lesson—more so indeed because of how bad it is, "for only what is wholly bad is implicitly charged with the immediate necessity of changing round into its opposite." "Spirit is all the greater, the greater the opposition from which it has returned into itself." Something of crucial significance is coming forth through this despicable endeavor: the necessity to integrate human mind and body. And of course none of that can be done justice to in a language of skulls and bones, but it's precisely the extremes of absurdity thus reached that will eventually generate the need of overcoming simpleminded observing reason (of which Hegel—perhaps unfairly—takes phrenology to be the culminating moment).[15]

The point is a fundamental one and will surface again; so I will take a moment to elaborate it further. Consider a sentence like:

(1) The sun rotates around the earth.

In the abstract—that is, independently of the circumstances in which it is uttered—we would think that (1) is false. But this abstract perspective is not endorsed by Hegel: if anything, *it* is a mistake for him. What is to find a place in Hegel's narrative is rather the concrete uttering and/or believing of (1) by some definite people or groups of people in a definite spatiotemporal context, and there is nothing false or wrong about *that*. Part of the task of the narrative, in fact, is to show that that concrete utterance and/or belief was exactly what *had to* happen then and there—and hence that it was exactly right that it happened, in the only sense of "right" that has currency here (more about this later). (Of course, it also had to happen that people would take abstract stances like the one we are opposing; so that "mistake" too, when looked at in the proper way, is/was just right.) In the terms of contemporary (analytic) philosophy of language, there is no in-

dependent room for falsity in Hegel's logic[16] because there is no independent room for sentences or propositions:[17] the unit of analysis
is always the whole speech act—where "whole" *really* means what it
says: an entirely self-sufficient context.

I must now address the third, and most troublesome, shape in
which contingency surfaces. It comes out in passages like the following:

> We must be content with what we can, in fact, comprehend at present.
> There is plenty that cannot be comprehended yet. (*Nature* 62)

> Even if, perhaps, the concept cannot yet give an adequate account of
> the "abundant variety" of nature so-called, we must nevertheless have
> faith in the concept though many details are as yet unexplained. (ibid.
> 359)

These statements fly in the face of the "absolute" claims with
which the present chapter began: it's not just a matter here of contingency being itself necessary, or of one not wanting to project too
much conceptual articulation onto earlier phases of the story—we are
being told, flat out, that the story is incomplete, that all sorts of details
in it still appear contingent *because we have not comprehended them yet*.
But, if that is the case, how could Hegel believe that he, or his
philosophy, was at the end of anything?

Once again, I will first approach this problem by trying to deflate
it. A certain amount of contingency is demanded by the externality
of nature, we know, but how much contingency that is might depend
on the progress of spirit. Things that at some point we take to be
contingent might later be recognized as traces of a superior rationality,
and then the blanket, uninformative clause, "There has to be some
contingency in nature, and this particular aspect of it falls within that
range," will give way to a more detailed, *concrete* account. Either phase
will have its totally comprehensive, retrospective story to tell, though
(as we should have expected) the later phase will have a better story
available, where the comprehensiveness is accompanied by more
structure (and where, incidentally, the earlier comprehensive story and
its necessity have been incorporated). But, if we can say all of that,
then surely Hegel can too: for a moment, he can take an external
point of view with respect to the (universally comprehensive) story
he is telling and announce that at some later stage a more articulate
(universally comprehensive) story will be available—that he *trusts* it
will be.

There is a lot of good sense to this modest proposal, but there is also an anything-but-modest—indeed, monumental—consequence of it: one with which we have been flirting for a while and to which it is now time to make a definite commitment. For, remember: within the current narrative no reference to the future is possible, hence if Hegel can "take an external point of view" within his text and make such references then his text *is not the narrative we are talking about.* This object we are facing—*whatever* ontology we assign to it: whether we think of it as a physical aggregate of paper, ink, and cloth, or as a type with many tokens, or as an editorially perfect "ideal" (not in Hegel's sense) of which those tokens are mediocre approximations—should not be confused with what I have been calling a story here. But what about the *meaning* the object conveys? Is that what the story is? Not in any straightforward sense, that is, not if the actual words used are to matter to this meaning; because then the latter would have to include (the meaning of) external comments like those quoted above—which, as we know, the story cannot include. The story metaphor has already been stretched beyond recognition; now we must give it the last push (realize the last *Aufhebung*?). We must finally make it clear that this story is not in words.[18]

In the *Science of Logic* we read the following:

> The divisions and headings of the books, sections and chapters given in this work as well as the explanations associated with them, are made to facilitate a preliminary survey and strictly are only of *historical* value. They do not belong to the content and body of the science but are compilations of an external reflection which has already run through the whole of the exposition and consequently knows and indicates in advance the sequence of its moments before these are brought forward by the subject matter itself. (54–55)

> Through . . . [the] progress [of the science], . . . the beginning loses the one-sidedness which attaches to it as something simply immediate and abstract; it becomes something mediated, and hence the line of the scientific advance becomes a *circle.* It also follows that because that which forms the beginning is still undeveloped, devoid of content, it is not truly known in the beginning; it is the science of logic in its whole compass which first constitutes the completed knowledge of it. (71–72)[19]

We are already familiar with the circular nature of Hegel's science, and in the next section I will take it up again. But for the moment let me just notice that the book *Science of Logic*—again, whatever the ontology of it—has no circular structure. In true Aristotelian fashion, it has a beginning, a middle, and an end; which suggests that the science of logic is not *what this book says*. Of what this book says the same holds as of its division in sections and chapters: it is an external compilation that is supposed to work as a Wittgensteinian ladder to help one reach the scientific viewpoint from which the true structure of the science can be fully appreciated. Logic moves in the pure, seamless medium of thought; and, however good a vehicle language might be for that movement, its residual empirical character must eventually be overcome.[20]

There is a profound and irremediable discrepancy between spiritual reality and anything that can be expressed in language: to access that reality we must overcome our very formulations of it, look past them much as one must look past a Greek sculpture if one is to see it as an incarnation of the idea.[21] To understand a proposition philosophically is also to explode it:

> The general nature of the judgment or proposition, which involves the distinction of subject and predicate, is destroyed by the speculative proposition, and the proposition of identity which the former becomes contains the counter-thrust against that subject-predicate relationship.— This conflict between the general form of a proposition and the unity of the concept which destroys it is similar to the conflict that occurs in rhythm between metre and accent. . . . The philosophical proposition, since it *is* a proposition, leads one to believe that the usual subject-predicate relation obtains, as well as the usual attitude toward knowing. But the philosophical content destroys this attitude and this opinion. (*Phenomenology* 38–39)[22]

So what the man Hegel uttered and wrote is only instrumental to the forming of a vision in which everything fits together; it prepares the stage for the imminent future when there will finally occur that comprehension of the past and present which cannot be given by any succession of distinct, *spaced* words and sentences and paragraphs. But it does *not* itself constitute that imminent future.[23]

There is more to be said about this operation and the (eternal) viewpoint it makes possible. But, before I turn to that further elaboration, I want to wrap up the present section with a brief summary of our main difficulty and a final remark.

It is indeed the case, I believe, that Hegel's occasional statements to the effect that some stuff will be better understood in some indeterminate future are best seen as external, *meta*narrative comments on the story he is in the process of unfolding. But that only makes them, at most, a little more external to the story than anything else he says—and indeed provides a vivid intimation of the externality *of the whole text*. "The story" relevant to Hegel is not just a universal one; it is also one spirit tells itself, in its perfectly transparent "language," and for that story what we read in Hegel's books (metacomments and all) is only useful groundwork. (Which also explains, incidentally, how that story can indeed be universal though no text of Hegel's—for all of his strenuous efforts—can claim to cover the whole thing.)

One last lesson we can learn from this discussion of contingency is that it would be wrong to conclude from Hegel's extreme rationalizing demands ("What is rational is actual; and what is actual is rational"[24]) that he was *forced* into the unrewarding task of proving the necessity of claims that were to be contradicted later by empirical findings. Those demands are compatible with resolving a given issue in a variety of ways; there is a substantial amount of play available to Hegel; his position does not stand or fall depending on the status of the specific paths he decided to take in individual cases. And, though there is a sense in which a commitment to Hegel is an all-or-nothing matter, this sense is definitely *not* that one cannot call oneself Hegelian without believing everything that is to be found in Hegel's *texts*.

3. Eternity

Consider my characterization of the universal story in Chapter 2. It was given as the limit of a process: of the gradual incorporation of every context, of everything external to the story that could provide a horizon for it, within the story itself. Imagine the effect that such a process will have on the temporality of the story—specifically, of *this* (kind of) story. To begin with, there will be chronological references in the story, which are necessary for it to make sense. A character's behavior, say, could not be understood (would not be "probable or necessary") unless one knew that he was living at the time of the Vietnam War—but the Vietnam War might be something the story does not talk about, so, *as a substitute for talking about it*, the story will contain some dates that help the reader insert its narrative into the larger picture of which she is *also* aware, and on the basis of which she will be able to judge the narrative's credibility.

But suppose now that the story grabs the Vietnam War, that the war becomes part of its plot. Then the dates will become irrelevant: the character's behavior can be justified by the story itself, without appealing to any external awareness. One might still have dates, of course, to reinforce the probability thus established and help the reader connect what she reads with her other contexts; but the first motivation is essentially redundant and will appear more and more so as the second one loses significance—as all contexts, not just the Vietnam War, are metabolized by the story. At the limit of the process, the place we are trying to make (liminal) sense of, it will be *only* redundant to say that something happened in 1967, because independently of that number (which gives, after all, a relational, positional determination: 1967 earth revolutions after some other thing happened[25]) we will know exactly why the incident had to turn out the way it did. Then chronology will fall off as a wasted, dried-out old skin, and the reptilian integrity of true historical development will emerge in all its vitality and robustness.

Consider the process from a different angle now: not the way it is originally anchored to, and gradually unmoored from, external time coordinates, but rather the way a temporal inner metric paces it throughout. Someone gets married, say, and then (we are told) so many weeks or months later his in-laws come to visit. Why do we need the specification of how many weeks or months that was? Because the author is relying on our externally acquired expectations of what tends to happen that long after a wedding to generate what reassurance or surprise she needs at this juncture. But, again, suppose now that she goes to work to minimize such a need for external reliance, in the converse direction from the one taken before: instead of reaching out toward more of the world, she reaches in toward a finer structuring of her subject matter. She doesn't just say, "Three weeks went by," and expect *us* to fill in what that implies: she *tells* us what it implies, in painstaking detail. The more she does that, the less the threeness of the weeks will matter: a metric space will not have to be superimposed on the information we are given—the information's topology will do the job, all by itself. That is, what things are adjacent to what others, and what are between what others, will become more and more all we need to know: the promissory note consisting of those earlier numerical distances will be paid off, not by an indeterminate outside to the story but by the story's very narrative unfolding.

"What spirit does is no history," Hegel says in *Religion* III: "Spirit is concerned only with what is in and for itself, not something past, but simply what is present" (232–33). And, again, "spirit is immortal; with it there is no past, no future, but an essential *now*" (*History* 79). "Chronological difference has no interest whatever for thought" (*Nature* 20). The point of view of absolute spirit, we know, is an eternal one ("Philosophy is no worldly wisdom, . . . but rather cognition of all that is eternal," *Religion* I 116–17); and in line with an old metaphysical and theological tradition Hegel understands this eternity not as everlastingness but as a(n eternal) present—indeed, an (eternal) instant.[26] There are three major components to his conception, as I see it, and the examples above were meant to be suggestive of the first one. So let us try to be more than suggestive: to bring it out in the open.

> Objects change, and the senses are aware of them in different ways. The changing is itself a sensible process, occurring in time. The sun exists: once it did not exist, some day it will not exist—all these states are external to one another in time. The being [of a thing] is *now*, and its nonbeing is separated from now; for time is what keeps the determinations apart from one another, external to one another. (*Religion* III 192)

"Now" *means to* refer to the context in which I am located, but the vanity of that reference had already surfaced for Kant—who had to rely on a mysterious *act* of synthesis to give it content.[27] For Hegel, no mystery is here to stay, and no irreducible conflict between the "faculties" of knowing and acting will be allowed: what follows instead is that the emptiness of the now makes the whole (allegedly) temporal structure of our experience explode. Now *when*? Is the now that is relevant to my action this minute, this day, the twentieth century, the epoch of humankind? (And, for that matter, is *here* this room, the United States, the solar system?) Just like demonstratives, dates give an impression of easy, obvious identification—most important, they make one feel that some event can be identified *as distinct from* some others, as external to them.[28] But the more I understand how subtly interrelated everything is with everything else the more I will realize that my now is all of history, that my present includes everything that is, that dates were only signposts for explanations yet to be given, that the real oppositions they *intended to* refer to were eventually to be resolved into ideal moments of one and the same integrated, organic account. Realizing that is tantamount to becoming emancipated from the chronological time that "keeps the determinations apart from one another, external to one another" and being left with (at most) *narrative* time: the *logical* succession of events in the overarching now.

> Time is the concept itself that *is there* and which presents itself to consciousness as empty intuition; for this reason, spirit necessarily appears in time, and it appears in time just so long as it has not *grasped* its pure concept, i.e. has not annulled time. It is the *outer*, intuited pure self which is *not grasped* by the self, the merely intuited concept; when this latter grasps itself it sets aside its time-form, comprehends this intuiting, and is a comprehended and comprehending intuiting. (*Phenomenology* 487)

The second element of Hegel's conception of eternity is an old but still superficial acquaintance, to which we need to devote more attention: the circular character of spirit's "progress." So take up ordinary stories once more, and suppose you are reading one of them, from beginning to end. As you proceed, the sense of relevance and the set of expectations ingeniously built by the author will drive you back and forth between discomfort and discovery, until some cathartic denouement is reached; but through all of these vicissitudes there will be clear dependencies established—some things will be (surprisingly) plausible because of what else has happened *before*. And now imagine that you don't put the book down after the first reading: you liked it so much that you want to go back to the beginning and experience it all over again. In this second visit, dependencies will acquire more of a symmetrical quality: when you encounter one of the hints that are supposed to enlighten you later, you will realize that its point is precisely that later enlightenment—that the *ground* for the suggestive detail is its eventual actualization. Imagine the limit of *this* operation: the understanding of the story you acquire after wading through it indefinitely many times. You can probably convince yourself that at that limit you would have overcome not just chronological but also logical priorities: that you would be facing a structure that is not just chronologically but also logically simultaneous—in which *tout se tient*, everything is in a relation of mutual necessitation with everything else.

I have already articulated the conceptual landscape in which spirit moves: its path is one of recognition, of establishing the internal consistency of a universal narrative while also appropriating it—coming to see it as *one's own*. The kind of rereading described above must be

placed in this landscape: both the consistency of the narrative and the
identification with all of it will emerge gradually, every step in the
process will also include an appreciation (however rudimentary) of
those two aspects, until the final culmination in *complete* recognition.
In that culminating, absolute state, spirit will be absolved not only
from the externality of time, but also from its successiveness: the eternal now will be a purely rational, *synchronic* vision.

And now for the third element. Begin with a quote:

> The subsistence of the community is its continuous, eternal becoming,
> which is grounded in the fact that spirit is an eternal process of self-
> cognition, dividing itself into the finite flashes of light of individual
> consciousness, and then re-collecting and gathering itself up out of this
> finitude—inasmuch as it is in the finite consciousness that the process
> of knowing spirit's essence takes place and that the divine self-
> consciousness thus arises. Out of the foaming ferment of finitude, spirit
> rises up fragrantly. (*Religion* III 233n)

What shows up in this passage is the same theme with which I
closed the last section: the story we read in any of Hegel's books is
but an intimation of the "story" that really matters—the one spirit
tells itself about itself. So let us develop this theme from the angle
that is relevant here.

Suppose I try to tell my story—Ermanno's, that is. I begin with a
date, August 2, 1950, with an environment already set, and with a
provisional list of few, scattered events; and then I proceed to extend
and deepen its fabric in two major ways. On the one hand, I connect
what was formerly scattered and add to it, until events follow "logically" from one another; but I also realize that beginning with a
particular date is an unwarranted, arbitrary move—that "my" story
begins before then, and that it includes the stories of all sorts of
"other" people. So I go on and on: I find that, to understand "what
I am," one has to bring in the internal Italian migrations of the 1940s
and 1950s, and then the delusional, ideologically constructed unifi-
cation of "my" country, and then again centuries of liberators running
through the South of that geographic expression of a peninsula, and
before I know it I am looking at the devastating consequences of the
decline and fall of the Roman Empire. Will I ever be able to articulate
all that is relevant—which is to say: all that is? To be more specific
about it: will the individual self-consciousness correlated with this
individual body ever be able to *tell* the universal, seamless narrative
into which "my" story is flowing? Of course not, but the more I

involve myself in this effort the more I *sacrifice* my individual integrity to that of a larger unit, hence the less obfuscated my vision is about what is "really" going on.

> If one holds fast to personality as an unresolved [moment], one has *evil*. For the personality that does not sacrifice itself in the divine idea is evil. It is precisely in the divine unity that personality, just as much as it is posited, is posited as resolved; only in appearance does the negativity of personality appear distinct from that whereby it is sublated. (*Religion* III. 194)

And, as my vision becomes less obfuscated, my individual, finite consciousness might receive a flash of the universal, infinitely detailed "story" of spirit—and *receiving that flash* amounts to *identifying* with such a story, seeing myself *as spirit*, seeing spirit as constituted precisely by infinitely many flashes like that.[29] If I focus on the specific words and mental occurrences that made the flash possible, I will have to think of them—as indeed we saw in the last section—as limited, empirical approximations to spirit's "eternal process of self-cognition" (however necessary it continues to be that such approximations be there, that the whole thing be indeed a sacrifice of my person, not a lapse of it into irrelevance). But I can also focus on the flash experience itself, and then I will realize that there is nothing limited about that: that the flash is the instantaneous accessing of spirit by spirit—and that spirit *just is* that instantaneous accessing of itself.

We have hit upon another intricate point, where a couple of reformulations might help. First, "people have been at pains to find the soul; but this is a contradiction. There are millions of points in which the soul is everywhere present; and yet it is not at any one point, simply because the asunderness of space has no truth for it" (*Nature* 352). It would be *almost* right to say that the soul is no less in one's elbows than in one's brain—except that people might take such a wording to imply the divisiveness which is usually ("naturally") associated with spatial locations. And that, of course, would be missing the mark: the soul in the elbows is the same as "the one" in the brain—indeed it is what makes the elbows and the brain one. Spirit has the same structure: its reality is to be found in infinitely many points, and yet all of those points are identical—*what* they make real is precisely their identity.

Second, Hegel distinguishes between the three moments of universality, particularity, and individuality in the concept (*Logic* 239), or, indeed, between these "*three* determinate concepts, . . . if one insists

on *counting* them" (*Science* 612), though of course "number is an un-
suitable form in which to hold conceptual determinations" (*Science*
612). That is, the concept is one-over-many (indeed, one-over-
everything), it is (infinitely) articulated, and it is actual, but all of
those aspects are firmly integrated with one another.

> Just as universality is immediately in and for itself already particularity,
> so too particularity is immediately in and for itself also *individuality;*
> this individuality is, in the first instance, to be regarded as the third
> moment of the concept, insofar as we hold on to its *opposition* to the
> two other moments, but it is also to be considered as the absolute
> return of the concept into itself, and at the same time as the posited
> loss of itself. (*Science* 612)

> The concept is . . . free subjective concept that is for itself and therefore
> possesses *personality*—the practical, objective concept determined in
> and for itself which, as person, is impenetrable atomic subjectivity—
> but which, none the less, is not exclusive individuality, but explicitly
> *universality* and *cognition*, and in its other has *its own* objectivity for its
> object. (*Science* 824)[30]

And, once again, spirit works the same way: each individual sacrificial experience just *is* the recognition of its identity with the single,
universal, supremely rational structure in all of its overwhelmingly
concrete richness of detail.

So, finally, this is how eternity is to be understood here: as an
instant in which the necessary interconnectedness of the absolute—
that is, of what is relative only to itself, absolved from any external
ties—flashes in a consciousness, which also recognizes itself in the
absolute. In that instant, time is not relevant, for three (related) reasons: (1) because the inter*connectedness* allows the consciousness ex-
periencing the flash to disregard any essentially demonstrative positional coordinates—all that is needed for the story to be understood
the story itself provides; (2) because the *inter*connectedness is reciprocal—everything grounds and is grounded by everything else, everything is beginning and end at once, so the very logical structure of
successive time is overcome; (3) because the flash is an appearance of
the whole thing at once—however painstakingly elaborate the path
might have been that made it possible.[31] An analytic logic would still
want to distinguish the consciousness having the instantaneous flash
from the identical thing that appears in every such experience and
would also want to distinguish every such experience from all others
(think of them as distinct examples of the same concept); but this is

dialectical logic, so one can say—*spirit* can say—that spirit's identity is the maximally dynamic superseding (*but not* canceling) of diversity that takes place when finite consciousnesses know themselves to be *identical with* the infinite. Every one of them is looking in the same mirror, and what it sees is itself.

4. The end of history

We seem to have tamed Hegel's totalizing claims. They are not to be understood, I argued, as incompatible with spirit taking novel, major strides in the future: they simply spell out an immanent feature of the kind of operation Hegel is conducting—they belong to the *logic* of that operation. What informative content they have is limited to communicating the satisfaction Hegel feels for a job well done, which again does not rule out indefinitely many yet-to-come (successful) performances of the same job. History only ends for Hegel in the trivial sense in which it always does, *wherever* one is located; for, wherever that is, that is exactly where the past comes to an end.

But it's not over yet. I suggested earlier that we don't just have here a smaller problem than ordinarily imagined, but (also) a different one; it's time now to flesh out that suggestion. And, in doing so, I begin with a straightforward and apparently extrinsic remark: clearly, the man Hegel does not just do a good job (if he does) of what specific task he is setting for himself—he thinks that other kinds of (intellectual) jobs, however in principle compatible with his own, are a ridiculous waste of time. Not that they are less necessary for being ridiculous, of course: they too have a place in the inflexible unfolding of his overarching narrative, so they too have important lessons to teach us. Spirit has to lose and even degrade itself before it can find its way. But ridiculous they are nonetheless. In the passage from the *Philosophy of Right* quoted at the beginning of this chapter, he mercilessly blasts at all utopian and normative thinking, calling it foolish and reducing it to cheap play with the phantoms of one's imagination.

If we forget the hype for a moment and focus on the sober facts of the matter, it seems that what Hegel says is obviously—once more, even trivially—true. Normative and utopian claims are about *what is not*, and not just because empirically it has not happened yet: of many empirically nonexistent occurrences we feel we can predict with absolute certainty that they will take place—they *already*, for all intents and purposes, belong to the world. With normative and utopian claims, however, something entirely other enters the scene: a world that is alternative to this one and may well never come to pass. So where does this world belong? What substantiates it? Nothing more, one might cynically (but, it seems, accurately) answer, than the fact that we *wish* it came to pass, and consequently think and talk about it. That is no less a fact than any other, of course; but there is no factuality to the *content* of our thoughts and talk. However elaborate they might be, and however consistent they might look, there is no way of knowing that any of it even makes sense.[32] One might not like to hear that, and might delude oneself with the pretense of an "objective" realm of values, a world of ideas that are more "real" than anything that *is* the case—but any such stance amounts to, indeed, wishful thinking, Hegel would say, and it is one more sad, *interesting* fact that people would fall for it.

So much for the sober truth. But the hype is there, too. Hegel does not just give us a taxonomy, he is also himself espousing implicit normative (!) claims. This stuff is not just deceptive and superficial and unwarranted: *one ought not to engage in it*. To repeat, the *Philosophy of Right* "shall [soll] be nothing other than an attempt *to comprehend and portray the state as an inherently rational entity*. . . . Such instruction as it may contain cannot be aimed at instructing the state on how it ought to be [wie er sein soll], but rather at showing how the state, as the ethical universe, should be recognized [wie er . . . erkannt werden soll]." It is not easy to reconcile normative pronouncements with Hegel's own logic—what I did above was to use some such "external" remarks as an Archimedean fulcrum around which to engineer a revolution in our understanding of the relation of Hegel's words to spirit's "story." But leave that aside now, and concentrate on the normative claims themselves: what Hegel is doing is denying any dignity or status to criticism—both the negative variety that consists of contesting the *validity* (never mind the truth) of what is, of passing a negative value judgment on it, and the positive variety of thinking up more desirable, rational, humane scenarios.[33] The only value judgment he will ever utter is one disqualifying all value judgments:

> There is no sin that cannot be forgiven, except for the sin against the Holy Spirit, the denial of spirit itself; for spirit alone is the power that can itself sublate everything. (*Religion* III 235)[34]

To put it bluntly, Hitler and Auschwitz can be forgiven, but one cannot forgive the "sin" of not forgiving them—of not seeing them as just another "probable or necessary" incident in the journey of all-sublating, all-incorporating spirit.[35]

> Moral claims that are irrelevant must not be brought into collision with world-historical deeds and their accomplishment. The litany of private virtues—modesty, humility, philanthropy and forbearance—must not be raised against them. The history of the world might, on principle, entirely ignore the circle within which morality and the so much talked of distinction between the moral and the politic lies. (*History* 67)

> [The Middle Ages offer] the most disgusting and revolting spectacle that was ever witnessed, and which *only philosophy can comprehend and so justify*. (*History* 382–83; italics mine)[36]

In the next chapter I will address this position in general terms. Here I am interested in bringing out its relevance to the subject matter at hand. For what we find when we travel along this road is an even more discouraging, despairing "end of history" than Hegel critics typically allege.

Normative and utopian claims are primarily addressed to the future. "You ought not to do this" implies that one hopes you *will* not do it; "you ought not to have done this" implies that one hopes you will not do it *again*, and in the meantime you *will* dissociate yourself from it. Even more naturally, the constructive proposals of "better" states or family structures or educational systems are phrased in a projectual mode—directed to an indefinite tomorrow. The reason is obvious: the future presents itself as open—precisely insofar as it is not—whereas the past is settled, closed. What is done cannot be undone.

And yet, this "obvious" view is not just mistaken, it is ideologically self-serving—which point, when spelled out, will force us to reconsider the "straightforward" remark above and the "sober truth" it invoked. For the past is not an impassive monolith, a depository of finished tasks, of fulfilled promises. There is a lot in the past that is not done (with)—a lot that is undone. Accepting the easy dichotomy between a solid, accomplished reality and the ephemeral play of thoughts and wishes about a possible future is already giving up, already denying such play any chance: disconnecting it from the soil from which it can draw nutriment and life. Not that it can ever be finally established that the play, *as play*, has a point—unless something does happen, we will never know that it could. But one can do better than that easy dichotomy: one can see cases of negative value judgments acted out in people's behavior, however destructive the outcome for their physical or psychological health; one can recognize the gesturing toward a more deserving society (or education, or religion, or . . .), and even the partial implementation of it—until of course it failed: if it didn't, there would be no need for a utopian thinking of it now. And one can derive confidence from so many witnesses, from so much clamoring.

But, for that to happen, we must think of the past, of history, as a repertory of diversity, in the specific sense of *projectual* diversity. We must see a lot going on there besides the official line: a multiplicity of false starts, of crushed hopes, of sidelined, forgotten dreams. And we must insist that, for all their being forgotten and sidelined and crushed, those projects are still there, and their presence *in the past* is an indictment of the official line—as much of a substantial incarnation of a normative stance on it as we can get but also, maybe, as much of one as we need. We must feel the cutting corners of the little rocks to which those (never realized) majestic boulders have been reduced, and sense that they can still draw blood.

Difference plays an essential role in Hegel's scheme of things; it is, after all, the engine driving spirit's movement. And it is not a difference spirit will ever (just) cancel: it will always be there, in all of its detail—spirit's "concreteness" is nothing else. But, though it's not annulled difference, it is colonized: turned into an ingenious way of making *this one* organism richer and stronger and more interesting and resourceful. The only difference that is left in the end is internal; the conflict that will continue to have currency is the one we remember—and we are so glad to have experienced. Every dissonant note must finally be resolved in a major chord—must function as a way of making that chord even more imposing and inevitable:

> Discords . . . need resolution. (*Aesthetics* 250)

> Along with the contradiction there is immediately given the necessity for a resolution of the discords. (*Aesthetics* 928)

And there is nothing more destructive for the significance of utopian or normative thought than this digestion of difference: this turning of sharp, pointed rocks into the pretty pebbles carried (and rounded, and made harmless) by an irresistible river. What we need from history to fuel criticism is its empirical, evenemental character, its turmoil, its messiness—its character *as history* precisely insofar as that opposes the establishing of any motif. Transforming history into a good story is really ending it: ending whatever use it might *still* have.

Except for one final irony (where "final," of course, is part of the irony). *As an empirical fact*, it looks as if the more people engage seriously in the kind of business Hegel endorsed—the more they try to silence the past in a sweet, murderous embrace—the more pointed and sharp history becomes: their ambitious goals, their *different, antagonistic*, ambitious goals (because there are so many of them, each trying to do "the same job" on everything—and everyone else), make for more clamor, draw more blood. And, correspondingly, the more people try to "do justice" to diversity, to leave room open for it, in the future and present and past, the more that diversity evaporates into bland, repetitive chitchat—once and for all, "really," colonized. The greatest sin, it seems, is not so much not to forgive, but rather to venture nothing that will ever need forgiveness.[37]

We can ask ourselves why that is, and to answer we will have to bring out again our understanding of such key terms as "narrative necessity," "speculative proposition," and "(dialectical) logic"—to appreciate some additional important lessons our unfolding of *their* semantic drift has been waiting to teach us. We know from Section 2 above that a speculative proposition is an oxymoron: speculation does not give us another kind of proposition, it *kills* proposition as such. And yet, there could be no speculation without some proposition to kill: if speculation is a superseding, there must be something to supersede—there must be an outside to speculation whose outsideness speculation can deny. No succession of spaced words and sentences and paragraphs, I pointed out later, will ever give us the vision Hegel is aiming at; that is why his "story" cannot be written (or told). But that vision is sacrificial in nature, hence a victim is needed: some spaced words and sentences and paragraphs must be there so as to suddenly be felt irrelevant, suddenly fall to the ground. Just as there must be an individuality so that it can be denied and identified with the universal. Just as, if substance is to be overcome by the maximally dynamic subject, substance must be present: no overcoming operation can occur without an object.

So the oxymoron "speculative proposition" is not to be finally discarded: if it went, speculation would go with it. And much the same is true of "narrative necessity": it too is an oxymoron, we realize now, but we need it to stay—and to stay that way. Any recognition of this necessity amounts to a collapse of the very dimensionality that makes narration possible—that makes it possible to tell one thing after another—since that recognition *is* the realization of how far these successive events hang *together;* but there would be no such realization if it did not apply to a narration.

As the concept has to wander into nature eventually to find itself in it, and as spirit is that very finding, so Hegel has to utter and write "external" words for the sublation that is philosophy, *and logic,* to take place. Typically, these words of his will be an invitation to dialectical dance: instead of settling into comfortable expectations, they will turn their subject matter inside out, make it unrecognizable before it can be truly recognized—before there can be something going on with that recognition, something dynamically happening. Whether it be a tragedy or a novel, a historical figure or an administrative office, a religion or someone else's philosophical work, it is typically the case that, when Hegel discusses it, it is hard to understand at first what he is talking about. Because of course he is desperately trying to talk past it. But there is no talking past all words; there is only silence there, and silence per se is no overcoming. What silence we are driving at is the one issuing when we finally "get it," but that is the outcome of a struggle with words—not of their sheer absence.

So it is precisely the fighting spirit of people like Hegel that can keep diversity in play: they *need* diversity so as to go to work on it. Those others who have peacefully "accepted" diversity have no use for it: no overcoming concerns them, they can rest safely on their side of every fence. And their words, however much they might invoke diversity, intimate no drama and afford no vision: they are but a constant, desperately consistent, nowhere-near-oxymoronic repetition of the identical.

FIVE

ECHOES AND COMPLAINTS

I said that a commitment to Hegel is an all-or-nothing matter—though (I added) that does not mean a commitment to every word the man wrote. What it does mean is that if you adopt Hegel's fundamental tool (and contribution)—dialectical logic—then no room is left for any radical disagreement with him. You may *mean to* disagree, of course, and even phrase acerbic criticism; but all of that can eventually be seen as yet another necessary phase of spiritual development. Your sin will be forgiven, whether you want such forgiveness or not—and even if you loathe it.

So I think that resistance to Hegel must be mounted, if it is to have any hope for success, at the very first step: against the immense seductiveness of narrative semantics.[1] And I think that such resistance is needed, for reasons that have already surfaced and that I will make fully explicit below. Since this is my attitude, I will commit (what Hegel would regard as) the ultimate monstrosity of throwing him into the battlefield of analytic logic—the logic of abstraction and separateness—and addressing his own logic in analytic terms. That implies, primarily, pulling this logic *apart*, making it into bits and pieces, and seeing how much there is that we can learn from, and even use, among those bits. It implies distinguishing dialectical logic from its "applications"—seeing it, against its own nature, as an organon that might or might not be brought to bear on various contingent matters. I will engage in this chainsaw massacre through most of the present chapter, and at the end of it I will address the issue of why I believe that the sawing is in order.

1. History of philosophy

I begin close to home—with internal professional concerns. So I hope that history will forever retain some of its empirical confusion, that it will not turn into the kind of "pat" apologue that (I noted in Chapter 3) conveys a strong feeling of unreality and, more disturbingly (I argued later), makes it impossible to use the past as an instrument of liberation. But there is an irony to the situation, as we have seen: confusion may be turned into the most powerful kind of order, the one to which no exception can even be contemplated; empirical side-by-sideness may be employed as the cheapest, but also stickiest, conceptual glue.

I believe that what I am proposing holds across the board within the discipline of history: that everywhere in it multiplicity should be earned through the bloody confrontation of bold (though also, of course, patiently and meticulously worked out) "visions"—that in no case do we gain real multiplicity by telling one damned thing after another. But I am going to leave history as such on the side here and direct my attention to that species of it which has a stable (if somewhat uneasy) presence within philosophy departments. Even more specifically, I am going to gloss over the archival and editorial work that infects the history of philosophy with empiricism—since that work can always be redeemed as a preliminary to conceptual accounts—and concentrate on what is a recurrent (and deeply un-Hegelian) feature of many such accounts: periodization.[2]

There are grandiose displays of this feature, occasionally alleging (a travesty of) an explanatory role—as when we hear that an author says such-and-such *because of* his modernity (or postmodernity, or premodernity, or whatever). But we can let such silliness fall of its own weight; what I am interested in, because I find it more dangerous for being superficially more plausible, is periodization as applied to a single author.

In *Nothing Is Hidden*, Norman Malcolm recites the conventional wisdom about Wittgenstein by saying that, in reading the *Tractatus* and the *Investigations*, "one becomes aware of a dramatic conflict between two radically different philosophical outlooks" (vii). Some writers, he continues, claimed that "when . . . [Wittgenstein] wrote the *Investigations* he no longer understood the *Tractatus*" (vii), but Malcolm (thank God!) is not going to go that far. He is only going to show the admirable way in which, in the *Investigations*, "Wittgenstein purged himself of the thinking of the *Tractatus* and created a revolutionary new philosophy" (ix).

The reference for this scatological language surfaces right away: Malcolm lists fifteen positions "taken in the *Tractatus* and rejected in Wittgenstein's later thinking" (viii). Since all of them amount to major philosophical theses, Aristotelian logic forces us to conclude that Wittgenstein the philosopher must be divided in two: an "earlier" and a "later." As for how and why these two philosophers inhabited the same person, the only possible answers must be external to the philosophers themselves: the person concluded that the first philosophy was a mistake, the person had some critical (revealing?) experiences, the person lost his mind (or regained it).

I have no special animosity toward Malcolm, and no special concern (here) with Wittgenstein. But I do think that, in the face of the obvious popularity of the periodization ploy, it helps to consider a Hegelian viewpoint on this matter. According to it, chronology is the limit of philosophical explanation—and, though this limit may well (contra Hegel) *be* there, one will never get to it if one stops too soon. So chronology as such should have no currency within philosophy, and (playing Kant on Hegel for a moment) the best methodological course is to act *as if* there always were a coherent stance associated with each proper name—to stick to the maxim "philosophi non sunt multiplicandi praeter necessitatem."

To be sure, the coherence invoked here will have most often (indeed, in virtually all cases worthy of attention) a dialectical character: it will be the kind that, far from being disarmed by contradiction, thrives on it. One will have to think of "a philosophy" not as defined by a collection of traits (in this case, specifically, a systematic collection of claims); for then the presence of traits *A* and not-*A* will automatically induce a branching into distinct collections and distinct philosophies. One will have to think of it instead as a live organism, which is alive precisely because (and insofar as) it goes any number of times from a given *A* to the corresponding not-*A*—indeed, finds it necessary for its own survival as the organism it is to go through such transformations. And one will not be too ready to call upon the correction of an earlier "mistake," or even to take too seriously an author's declaration to that effect; for, again, from this viewpoint nothing is just a mistake. *A* had to occur when it did and had to be "corrected" later, and replaced with its opposite—and whoever forfeits the task of accounting for the rationality of that development, for how the development is conceptually, not empirically, grounded, is at that very moment stepping outside the discipline of philosophy.

The Italian neoidealist philosopher (and Mussolini's minister of education) Giovanni Gentile theorized the identity of history, philosophy, and the history of philosophy.[3] As an adolescent, I lived some of the practical consequences of this Hegelian stance: in the Italian Liceo, after Gentile's "reformation" of it, a single teacher taught (only) history and philosophy, and the philosophy he/she taught was the history of philosophy, and some especially enthusiastic enforcers of this plan fantasized of a history of philosophy (and a history, period) that contained no proper names—that consisted of the logical progression of the idea. I don't share the easy optimism that most often accompanies such views, but I recognize the independent legitimacy of an intellectual endeavor that proceeds under the constraint of never referring in an essential manner to that (chronological) time which "keeps the determinations apart from one another"—and hence must understand any such reference as a failure. I find that, when I am involved in this endeavor, I tend to simply lose interest if some momentous turnaround in a philosopher's development is attributed to his falling under the influence of X, or having his previous research project come to a dead end, or being enlightened on the way to Damascus—all of these "explanations" feel irrelevant, seem to be category mistakes. And, yes, I also have a tendency (because I "fell under the influence" of Gentile's theories and practices early?) to think of this endeavor as most properly conceptual, and as having most of a right of currency within philosophy. Though of course there is no reason to share that tendency—and even those who don't can still appreciate what can be gained by doing one's best to forever turn chronology into narrative.

2. Discursive strategies

As was suggested in the last paragraph (and, indeed, as has been known for a while), Hegelian reconciliation does not stop at the boundaries of an individual author's life. Not just Wittgenstein or Kant should not be divided into an earlier and a later, a precritical and a critical; any opposition between two "distinct" philosophers must also be *aufgehoben*. Nothing any philosopher said—however absurd it might sound—should ever be left out in the cold; all of it must eventually find its way home. This theme emerges in every phase of Hegel's career, from his early Young-Turkish polemical pieces to his late-day monumental pedagogy:

> True speculation can be found in the most divergent philosophies, in philosophies that decry one another as sheer dogmatism or as mental aberration. The history of philosophy only has value and interest if it holds fast to this viewpoint. For otherwise, it will not give us the history of the one, eternal reason, presenting itself in infinitely manifold forms; instead it will give us nothing but a tale of the accidental vicissitudes of the human spirit and of senseless opinions. (*Difference* 114)

> The general result of the history of philosophy is this: in the first place, that throughout all time there has been only one philosophy . . . ; in the second place, that the succession of philosophic systems is not due to chance, but represents the necessary succession of stages in the development of this science. . . . The latest philosophy contains . . . those which went before. (*Philosophy* III 552)

But the strategy has important applications outside philosophy (if there is any such thing—which in a way is the whole point); and to these "other" applications I want to turn now.

Imagine two fierce intellectual opponents engaged in a heated debate. One is (say) vehemently defending the justice of a minimal state; the other is just as vehemently arguing that no justice can be at hand unless important public services are available to the poor and destitute. If the two interlocutors are committed to Aristotelian logic, they must think of what they are involved in as a zero-sum game: they hold positions that are incompatible with one another, hence it is impossible for both of them to be right (though they might both be wrong), hence the only way for one to win the argument is to make the other lose it. The tactics most naturally associated with this conception of the engagement are destructive—in two (related) senses.

First, there is no point in leaving the opponent standing, in salvaging him, because, again, one takes the opponent to be wrong and there is no point in salvaging a wrong view. There may be elements of it worth salvaging, but only if they can be severed from their context as that context is exploded; and what definitely one must not attempt to salvage, in any case, is the *integrity* of the opponent—for such integrity is a threat to one's own. Second, one need not fuss about the level of sophistication of one's attacks: a cheap shot may be just as deadly as an artful one—and, if it is, it works just as well. A trivial inconsistency among the opponent's most superficial claims will do the job as much as an elaborate critical study of some remote (inconsistent) implications of those claims: given what "the job" is, if you are lucky enough to hit upon the former it would be silly to keep looking for the latter.[4] Thus, on the one hand, you will be inclined to take no prisoners and, on the other, you will show respect for the complexity of the other guy's position only if you absolutely have to—whereas, if you can, you will blow it up wholesale.

But suppose that one of these guys is Hegelian. Then he cannot think of his "opponent" as being wrong, or indeed as being really "other": looking at that person is like looking at himself in a mirror— a distorting mirror, maybe, but still such that he can get from it an interesting perspective on himself. Winning the argument for him will amount to incorporating the interlocutor's position: proving it to be an early, somewhat rudimentary, version of "his own" (that is, of the position which he *now* has—but which is still *the same* position as the interlocutor's, the result of a "maturing" of it). And it will also amount, Hegel would say, to him for the first time really *having* a (stable) position—as opposed to a capricious, fleeting "opinion," easily stated and just as easily contradicted:

> Actuality is that which is effective and sustains itself in its otherness, whereas the immediate still remains liable to negation. (*Right* 116)

Two major consequences will follow from adopting this stance. First, there will be no "abstract" disregarding of *any* details in the opponent's view. Its strengths will be played up, as the best starting points for identifying with it; but the weaknesses will have a major role too, even the inconsistencies—they will give evidence that this view is indeed in the process of turning into its opposite, that is, into the later version of the same position one now holds. Benevolent attention will be directed at all such details, because in focusing on them one is retracing one's own path, intellectually reappropriating one's own history, and there will be a soothing, conciliatory flavor to such rediscovery of earlier "false" steps, of long-forgotten "lapses." Nor is it just that everything the other says will matter, in a distributive sense: the whole thing collectively understood will have to be saved. One will not just want to adapt the elements of the other's view to one's own (different) goals; that entire view, with all of its structure, will have to find a place in oneself, be recognized as a form of life whose value and significance one can understand and appreciate, and has in fact oneself experienced—once.

Second, the task one will be facing is constructive. The point is emphatically not to be the last man standing, because canceling the alternative *without preserving it* would count as a failure; what one must do instead is studiously weave a net of connections with that alternative, bridge anything that might look like an impassable chasm with ingenious "mediations." It will take a lot of crafty storytelling to confer plausibility on the claim that (say) a supporter of tax revolt, by just pursuing the destiny of his own tenets, *must* end up espousing the welfare state—but nothing less than that amount of craftsmanship is required here.

A sympathetic way of describing these Hegelian moves would be to say that they, more than their Aristotelian counterparts, tend to promote agreement.[5] But that description may be *too* sympathetic, and to see why imagine now that both interlocutors play by Hegelian rules. As it turns out, there are two ways this can happen: one of them does indeed favor agreement, but the other instigates an even more devastating (because more devious) form of disagreement *and abuse*.

It is possible that the interlocutors regard their very confrontation as a moment of dialectical crisis—in particular, that each thinks of either position as bringing out elements of weakness in its opposite. Then each will believe that both positions are limited and must be superseded in a higher unity that does justice to both, and from whose viewpoint both will be seen as necessary, but equally temporary, earlier phases of itself. This attitude will foster genuine harmony: the benevolent, caring attention each participant pays to the details of the other's position will have a solid base in the equal dignity they assign to each other. But note that it's not going to be easy to even qualify such an attitude as Hegelian; to do so, one would have to utilize in a substantial manner the inside/outside distinction discussed in Chapter 4. From *within* a Hegelian view, we know, it doesn't even make sense to think of a (more) harmonious *future;* so one would have to think of the interlocutors as retrospectively projecting such harmony from a place spirit has not reached yet—a story that has not yet unfolded.

A much more straightforward Hegelian reading of the situation, and a much more likely development of it, would have the participants try each to incorporate the other's position in *his own*, so that what looked like benevolence turns ugly. Colonization, political or otherwise, offers the best examples of this kind of "exchange": the colonizer is often tenderly affected as he finds traces of his own childhood among the "primitives" he is in the process of "civilizing,"[6] but "primitive" is not a value-free term, and not one practically harmless either—once you start throwing it around, appropriate behavior will soon follow. Or, maybe, throwing it around is an appropriate excuse for otherwise inexcusable behavior; Hegel himself is a good instance of this practice.

> Negroes are to be regarded as a race of children who remain immersed in their state of uninterested *naivete*. They are sold, and let themselves be sold, without any reflection on the rights or wrongs of the matter. (*Mind* 42)

> The original inhabitants of America . . . are a vanishing, feeble race. It is true that in some parts of America at the time of its discovery, a pretty considerable civilization was to be found; this, however, was not comparable with European culture and disappeared with the original inhabitants. . . . The natives of America are, therefore, clearly not in a position to maintain themselves in face of the Europeans. (*Mind* 45)

> America has always shown itself physically and psychically powerless, and still shows itself so. For the aborigines, after the landing of the Europeans in America, gradually vanished at the breath of European activity. (*History* 81)

> We may conclude *slavery* to have been the occasion of the increase of human feeling among the Negroes. . . . Slavery is itself a phase of advance from the merely isolated sensual existence—a phase of education—a mode of becoming participant in a higher morality and the culture connected with it. Slavery is in and for itself *injustice*, for the essence of humanity is *freedom*; but for this man must be matured. (*History* 98–99)

When looked at from this point of view, the discursive and argumentative strategies I am describing appear as confrontational as their analytic counterparts (or more)—though also, of course, differently so. Whereas an Aristotelian working out of intellectual antagonism ordinarily issues in attempts at destroying the opponent, its Hegelian alternative will most often aim at *using* him: making his very opposition into more interesting substance (more "concrete" content) for the development of one's view. And, since two can play this game, the winner will be the one who succeeds in "constructively" incorporating the other in his own biography—or who has more guns to back up his story.[7]

The scenario that surfaces by following up such suggestions might seem reminiscent of more Nietzsche than Hegel: of a reality consisting of irreducibly conflictual narratives, each trying to extend its "will to power" over the others ("What does not kill me makes me stronger"). And, indeed, this Nietzschean picture is relevant to Hegel's own production; for, while each of Hegel's texts claims to present us with (part of) a comprehensive, (dialectically) coherent account, such accounts are not coherent (dialectically or otherwise[8]) with one another—many important matters of detail are resolved differently in different texts.[9] So, one might say, there is genuine competition acted out between these texts, and of course each of them (insofar as it claims to be comprehensive) would also have to be thought of as implicitly claiming to have room within itself for all the others. Then Nietzsche might be seen as offering "the truth of" Hegel: the self-conscious appreciation of a conflict that "in itself" was already there. (Which in turn is a good example of how seductive Hegelian logic is: how its retrospective stance can conquer even the future, and future opponents—*after* they have happened.)

At any rate, whether you decide to go with Hegel's phase of spirit or with some later, more explicit and developed one, you will have available the incestuous conversational techniques I have been talking about—and will put them to good use to the extent that you treat your opponents as means rather than ends, and "naturalize" them as necessary obstacles for the better flourishing of yourself.

3. Living in the wake of incarnation

There is a flip side to the incest I have just described. The instrumental naturalization of other spirits goes hand in hand with a spiritualization of nature. We can get to the latter by reflecting on the central dogma (and mystery) of the Christian religion: the incarnation. Before that event, the world was impious and dumb, forlorn and wretched; there was a radical opposition between its meaningless, sinful inertia and the import of God's will. Which also explains why that will had to manifest itself as constraining, as reproachful, as irate. Then Christ happened, and things were never the same again:

> Religion offers a possible reconciliation with nature viewed as finite and particular. The original possibility of this reconciliation lies in the

original image of God on the subjective side; its actuality, the objective side lies in God's eternal incarnation in man, and the identity of the possibility with the actuality through the spirit is the union of the subjective side with God made man. (*Faith* 180–81)

From then on, nature was sacred—all of it was—and Fichte (among others) is chastised for not recognizing this: for continuing to think of nature in oppositional terms, as a resistance to be annihilated, an enemy to be vanquished.

[Fichte's attitude] presupposes an utterly vulgar view of nature and of the relation of the singular person to nature. This view is one which is denuded of all reason, for the absolute identity of subject and object is entirely alien to it, and its principle is their absolute non-identity. So it can only comprehend nature in the form of the absolute opposite, and hence as a pure object with respect to which it is only possible either to be dependent on it, or to make it dependent upon oneself. . . . That nature is something absolutely unhallowed and lifeless, that it is nothing in itself, and exists only in connection with an other—this is the vulgar, teleological principle . . . [of] Fichte's philosophy. (*Faith* 176–77)

What does this all mean, once we translate it from the picture-thinking of the philosophy for the masses (of religion, that is[10]) into perspicuous conceptual language? Picking up where we left off at the end of Chapter 2, it means that, if the (one) concept is the absolute, then no aspect of reality is without conceptual dignity: every such aspect belongs with the concept, at *its* level, doesn't just "fall under" it but provides a meaningful articulation of it. A world that is penetrated by the Holy Spirit, in which God has found His home, is also one in which every little thing expresses God and deserves as much attention as any big thing. This is what Kant (another major culprit) missed, and what much lesser people have manifested in their instinctive behavior:

The defect of Kant's philosophy consists in the falling asunder of the moments of the absolute form; . . . our understanding, our knowledge, forms an antithesis to being-in-itself. . . . But . . . thought had spread itself over the world, had attached itself to everything, investigated everything, introduced its forms into everything, and systematized everything, so that on every hand thought-determinations had to be followed. . . . And therefore in theology, in governments and their legislation, in the object aimed at by the state, in trades and in mechanics, it is said that men ought to act according to universal determinations, i.e., rationally: and men even talk of a rational brewery, a rational brick-kiln, etc. This is the requisite of concrete thought; while in the Kantian result . . . an empty thought was alone present. (*Philosophy* III 478)

Abstractive understanding will think of natural entities as irrelevant examples of the concept: what belongs to them that does not belong to the concept has no place in an intellectual domain, it is destined to the lowly, contemptible status of a trivia question. But if the concept lives in the world, if the latter is what provides its texture and content, then suddenly everything matters, from everything we can derive invaluable *logical* lessons. Any number of (progressively less recognizable) Hegelian grandchildren have drawn out the enormous dividends of adopting this stance—often biting on their ancestor's hand as they did so. To limit ourselves to this century, how shall we otherwise understand Benjamin's careful unpacking of mechanical reproduction or Barthes's rigorous analysis of (the language of) fashion (which the master himself, we know, might not have approved of—possibly against his better judgment[11]), Adorno's *Minima Moralia* or Eco's *Diario minimo*? How shall we account for the fact that they found it intellectually rewarding to scrutinize such matters, and expected their scrutiny to enrich their comprehension, if not by referring to a concept that is no longer sitting in heaven but walks among us, and that we must be ready at any moment to recognize?[12] (Will we miss Christ again, and crucify him a second time, if he came back?)

4. Promises, promises

A major advantage of an abstractive approach, when it comes to identifying something, is that it makes it possible to disconnect the thing (including the important case in which the thing is oneself) from all sorts of occurrences it is involved in, and to think of such incidents as not touching its essence—as leaving it "essentially" unscathed. What that essence comes down to gets to be phrased more and more in terms of potentialities: Descartes's wax *is* nothing but what it *can be*. When pressure is applied to the Aristotelian paronymy (?) between potential and actual being, the latter (despite Aristotle's own statements to the contrary) shows a perplexing tendency to collapse into the former.

For the specific case of human behavior, potentiality can be phrased in terms of promise: the explicit act of committing oneself (publicly or not) to some intention, or the implicit inclination unconsciously displayed by early moves ("this kid shows promise as a fullback"). And "promise" is an interesting term here, given that it also refers to the archetypal performative; so that what we are, it is suggested, is to be cashed out not in the larger context of what we do, but rather in the more limited one of what we do *with words*. Practical consequences of this general attitude can be found all over. A person's love for another, say, is claimed to be independent of how much he hurts her: every time that happens, there is an external reason for it—and one to be disregarded when trying to understand what the guy is *really* all about. Whether someone is a decent citizen or not should not be decided on the basis of his various ugly misdeeds—one often finds oneself in tight spots, where not too many options are left and one is (contingently) forced to act against his natural inclinations. And then there are those, of course, who know perfectly well that they have superior gifts—except that the circumstances are not right, they were not born at the right time, they are not receiving the right response, or whatever.

All the above can, and often will, be regarded as pitiful excuses. But here I am less interested in blaming them than in pointing out that the opening up of a logical space for such excuses and the undecidability of the issue of when they are legitimate (which makes them much more effective, if still pitiful) are obvious consequences of the analytic mode of thinking. As long as it is possible to dislocate what one is from what one does—or, for that matter, from anything at all that "happens" to one—and as long as what one is must be found in some identical structure that persists through innumerable confusing vicissitudes, there will have to be room for possibly finding oneself in a vague and fuzzy structure. And, if the room is there, we will use it, because vague and fuzzy structures can serve us well: they will not be easily impacted by conflicting data, including negative data about ourselves.

In contrast with this comforting openness, a Hegelian attitude is mercilessly strict: if you want to know what you are, look at what you do—at *all* you do. In particular, don't delude yourself by discarding your (outer) behavior as not necessarily correlated with your (inner) character; for that character is at best a seed whose reality will prove itself by growing into a definite plant, luxuriant or stunted as it may be—and *then* we will know what it was the seed of.

There is, of course, a difference between what someone means and
what he says; but science is not concerned with what someone means
in his head, but with what he says. (*Religion* II 260)

A person's decency, or her intelligence, or her love of another will
be found not in the privacy of a transparent contact with herself ("*I*
know what *I* am about; all you ever see is my outside shell"), but in
the multifarious goings-on of her existential path.[13] A promise was
earnest only if it is fulfilled;[14] if it isn't, and it felt like it was earnest,
it will be interesting to consider why that self-deception arose. For,
after all, "spirit is what manifests itself, what appears but is infinite in
its appearance; spirit that does not appear *is not*" (*Religion* I 120).

Freud's psychoanalytic practice is the most influential development
of this aspect of Hegelian logic—down to the detail (as we will see)
of using awkward, oxymoronic phrases to signal the necessity of an
Aufhebung. Independently of what we (sincerely) declare, we are told
there, our behavior is most often determined by unconscious wishes
and intentions; and if one wants to know what those unconscious
factors are one should simply look at the behavior itself, at all of its
complex fabric—never disregard anything as irrelevant, or unimpor-
tant, or the result of a random "external" disturbance, but rather take
it all seriously, put it all together, and see what story it is trying to
tell us. Some of us might wish that Freud had not couched this sensible view by talking about "unconscious intentions" and might feel
like pointing out that intentional behavior is what we are responsible
for—and the reason why we are responsible for it is that we consciously chose it. So, one might think, whatever important feature of
Oedipus is revealed by his act of killing his father, it would be unfair
to call that feature intentional. I will say more in a minute about this
unfairness; now I just point out that "unconscious intention" is precisely one of those expressions through which, in Hegel's scheme of
things, spirit is recognizing the necessity of overcoming the whole
explanatory scheme of intentions, individual self-consciousness, *and*
individual responsibility. In using expressions like that, Freud is revealing (unconsciously?) the intimate Hegelian structure of his framework.

But can we go this far? If the former extreme was pitifully self-
serving, isn't this one absurdly demanding? Surely I did not "really
mean" a promise that, as soon as I uttered it, I proceeded to smother
in sloth; but what about genuine external impediments, unexpected
contingencies over which I had absolutely no control? Can I still say

that the plant will prove the value of the seed if someone shoots me from the next car on the freeway as I am diligently doing my best to make it to the appointment I committed myself to?

Hegel has answers for such questions, and we know what they are. "My" life does not begin or end with the formation and decay of this body, nor does the promise I entail. I will only ever get partial, misleading results concerning the significance of what "I" do if I refuse to sacrifice my integrity to that of the whole thing. The promise we are talking about is not (just) one I made: it is one spirit made, through me, and when we attempt to find out, by looking at (among other things) my subsequent destiny, what the promise was worth, we are not trying to *limit* (God forbid!) the promise's scope of relevance to something this person (or body) is responsible for. We are trying to establish what *spirit* was up to.

At this point, one might feel understandably dizzy. The sensible recommendation of not resting content with what one says about oneself, but considering carefully how what he does fits with his declarations of intent, has been pushed so far that we seem to have lost the reason why we were going through all of this in the first place. For we no longer have a person who does and says anything: we are left with the universe showing what it "meant" by its next "moves." If this air is too thin for us to breathe, we might find consolation in the intermediate position Kant offers, in the *Religion within the Limits of Reason Alone*:

> [A man] can gain . . . confidence . . . [in his moral disposition], without yielding himself up either to pleasing or to anxious fantasies, by comparing the course of his life hitherto with the resolution which he has adopted. It is true, indeed, that the man who, through a sufficiently long course of life, has observed the efficacy of these principles of goodness, from the time of their adoption, in his conduct, that is, in the steady improvement of his way of life, can still only *conjecture* from this that there has been a fundamental improvement in his inner disposition. Yet he has reasonable grounds for *hope* as well. (62)

It's not to say that Kant's position, when it is itself pushed to its ultimate consequences, is much more reassuring for one's sense of one's own integrity than Hegel's.[15] But, for the specific issue we are currently dealing with, his recommendation does not entail as great a loss—of ourselves as individually responsible or even of our intentions. We can continue to talk about the latter, Kant would grant, as long as we don't take that talk as definitive of anything. The language of intentions is itself a promise, which one forever attempts to fulfill by looking at concrete, "external" behavior. It is never conclusively clear what that behavior proves—how much of it is revealing our will and how much is a case of nature working itself out through us. But there is a place to be found amidst these negotiations for the coherent thought of individual responsibility, impossible as it is to give that thought empirical substance. Whereas any such place is denied in the universal fusion issuing from the Hegelian sacrifice.

5. The voice of nothing

At the beginning of the *Science of Logic*, in a passage discussed in Chapter 3, Hegel shows how the two most radically opposed concepts of being and nothing turn out to be identical. What follows, in that work and then throughout the *Encyclopaedia*, is a detailed belaboring of the identity: nothing (or negation) organizes being internally, until at the end we find ourselves contemplating an infinitely articulate structure where a maximum of freedom coexists with a maximum of necessity—everything in it is what it must be, *and* everything follows its own law; there is *nothing* outside that structure which can even conceivably have any impact on it. Empty being has become an immanent God, totally autonomous as the God of Christian theology is supposed to be but also so thoroughly, intimately comprehensive of His other as to put virtually any (other) religious view to shame for its cowardice.

Much of post-Hegelian philosophy can be seen as a reaction to this suffocating view: as a series of dedicated attempts to speak in the name of that nothing which the latter denied, enslaved to the project of structuring being, and finally claimed to have "resolved" in the universal theodicy of the concept.[16] Nothing, of course, is precisely the *non*concept: what resists making sense, being integrated in a good story—the anomaly, the exception, the element of unclever, obtuse subversion. And the voice of nothing is (to begin with) one of protestation, of blame, of resentment; it passes a judgment on all that is, however necessary it might be; it evokes "another" rationality, another necessity—one that continues to be necessary despite the fact that it is not actual, with all the irritating, inspiring force of a deontic modality. It is the voice of justice, of morality, of that otherworldly good which dialectical logic had enabled Candide *redivivus* to sneer at.

Over one and a half centuries, resistance to Hegelianism has taken (understandably) a variety of forms—so many indeed that it is difficult to recognize the common patterns. What I intend to do now is bring out the most general such patterns, as a premise for finally stating my view on how we should "deal with" Hegel today.

First, explicit awareness of *whom* one was resisting has progressively faded. Hegel looms large in Kierkegaard's rehabilitation of the locus of agonizing individuality, but Nietzsche's concerted attack on systematic thinking is surprisingly reticent about him; and in the twentieth century's revamping of immediacy—whether it be the phenomenological data of Husserl or the laboratory protocols of neopositivism—it typically sounds as if Hegel never existed. Then, in a move that ironically mimicked Hegel's own stance, Heidegger (re)launched the fad of sitting in the imminent future of philosophy as such—a future populated by philosophy's ruins, the outcome of its "destruction"—thus lumping the owl of Minerva together with the all and sundry, and effectively disguising what the real problem was.[17]

The uncanny practical counterpart of this forgetfulness is that dialectical thinking has never been more powerful—*now, after* the demise of what presented itself as its incarnation on earth. Self-satisfied contemplation of the workings of "the system" (that is, the market), and of its superior rationality, has drowned all utopian thinking—indeed, there are caricatures of intellectuals out there preaching an all-too-Hegelian "end of history." The traditional opposition between morality and self-interest is being brilliantly *aufgehoben* by reconstructing the former within "rational" decision theory—and thus, Hegel would say, positing their identity, having them recognize themselves in their other. Individual humans and cultures are metabolized within a universal melting pot (the new phase of spirit?) that acts at a scale they have no hope of even understanding—let alone controlling, or fighting—and where "consciousness" and "memory" are redefined as the imaging conducted by *the one and only* Internet, and by the inexhaustible data banks "it" has access to. And rebelling against all of this is regarded as a sign of immaturity, of a dangerous enthrallment before one's fanciful opinions, of an incapacity to "comprehend one's time in thoughts." It is less than a wrong attitude, or than a fruitless or even counterproductive one: it is vain.

It is quite possible that none of this is the intellectuals' fault—that the wheels they spin are not attached to anything. But that is not how an intellectual *ought to* see it; so I consider it a duty to bring out a second major feature of post-Hegelian reactions—and one that

might very well have made the despicable developments above easier
to unfold. In going against Hegel, too many people have left him too
much room and confined themselves to operating within the narrow
confines left by an implicit acceptance of his claims. They left being
alone and had nothing speak all by itself; they quickly consigned the
world to the opposition (which knows how to keep itself busy di-
gesting it) and painstakingly tried to articulate radical otherness, un-
compromising difference—sometimes deriving "a gloomy satisfaction" from "such sentimentalities" (*History* 21). They settled for a
status as pure and beautiful souls (untainted by the corrupted bodies
they often inhabited)—and you know how it goes with souls like
that (Hegel certainly did): what they are trying to make themselves
different from couldn't care less, indeed has no trouble turning them
into exotic curiosities, well-kept tenants of a colorful zoo. Occasionally, there will be clear signs of this amused indifference, and of the
consequent successful colonization—as when the emblem of apoca-
lyptic, exorbitant difference is used to confer a touch of class on a
major motion picture.[18]

But there is something else one can do: one can play a game of
reciprocity with Hegel—put his infinitely complex and coherent being at the service of an articulation of nothing. Negation, however
radical it is to be, need not paralyze itself in Promethean apartness
(and in the impenetrable, if prophetic, style that usually accompanies
it); and criticism need not reduce to the Socratic practice of subvert-
ing positions from the inside and making them uselessly fall apart.
Indeed, if they reduce to that, negation and criticism are likely not
to have much effect: in the absence of alternatives, one will always
be allowed to think of one's position—however convincing the objections against it—as the least of evils. The most effective way of
questioning what is, in all of its rich interconnectedness, and of exposing the story-character of its inevitability, consists of telling *other*
stories, other *examples* of what can issue from one and the same narrative, rationalizing practice, as articulate and "probable" as the official
one is, and in the course of doing so raising the ever-threatening
specter of a "Why not?" question, sharpening the urgency and relevance of a demand for justification, realizing the dignity of justification as such.

I suggested at the end of Chapter 4 that, as a matter of fact, the
best cure for Hegel might be more, *much* more, of the same; the
implication here is that abandoning his line of business in his hands
is a truly defeatist choice, that one can only fight him by displaying

the same arrogant ambition, and shooting for the same universal comprehensiveness, as he does. I happen to believe that, though this operation can be conducted in a community, with different members of
it incarnating different varieties (and outcomes) of overweening pride,
it can also be conducted within an individual subject—precisely because the subject is not in-dividual.[19] The subject, that is, can be the
theater of (a dialogue among) conflicting spirits, all pursuing their
destinies with the same relentless conviction and yet presenting with
their very plurality obtrusive "empirical" limits, "recalcitrant,"
opaque givens to one another. The conflict of faculties can graduate
into a conflict of Hegelian overarching narratives: of radically *distinct*
narratives, which manifest this distinctive character (give it "being-
for-itself") by the healthy resistance they continue to exercise against
successful incorporation, the intellectual resources they surprisingly
throw at their greedy opponents, the unexpected variants they find
for the beaten path.

Taking this course amounts to splintering Hegel—reducing him to
bits. Turning his absolute idealism into a heuristic stance that helps
promote even more irreducible—because more "concrete," more articulate—division than traditional analytic logic could ever allow for.
In the previous sections of this chapter, I have suggested an even finer
splintering of him into even smaller bits—a collapsing of his powerful
voice, of the rich harmony of that voice, into faint, monotonic ech-
oes: "Hegelian" therapy, "Hegelian" conversational techniques, "Hegelian" analyses of cultures, even a "Hegelian" way of reconstructing
the intellectual biography of an author. So I have been doing what I
promised at the beginning of the chapter: forcing dialectical logic to
play by the rules of its analytic counterpart, refusing the logic of the
total story *while simultaneously* proving it to be (locally) effective.[20] It
is time now to explain why I think that this "monstrous" practice is
in order.

Analysis breaks apart. It hurts, it is destructive, it is allied with
death. It takes things out of context, leaves most of their reality un-
attended to, "changes the subject" in ways that are disrespectful of its
integrity. It is, Hegel would say and I would agree, evil. And yet, I
don't see how freedom is possible without this evil. Not the "freedom" that consists of intellectually submitting to the necessity of one's
situation—as a preliminary, or a reinforcement, for more substantial
forms of submission. But the modest, precious, empirical freedom of
play: the amount of play each of us has, the little bit of discretion we
can sometimes use. This discretion is obtained through disconnect-

edness, through severing a link here and there—and of course when
we sever such links we are guilty, at the very least of losing touch
with where we are, of no longer "comprehending" it, and we end
up (to some extent) in empty space, helplessly flapping our wings like
Kant's proverbial dove,[21] having lost those ties through which any of
our thoughts and talk "make sense." Except that we, as a matter of
obtrusive fact, do not want to comprehend too much, there are things
we do not want to comprehend, we want to be free *of them*—such
is the freedom that matters. And this freedom we gain by abstracting,
cutting off, taking out of context, violating. Without this freedom—
and the responsibility it demands, the evil it requires us to assume
upon ourselves—being will close smoothly over us, snap shut, as-
phyxiate us with the nightmare of a perfect fit, of a watertight seal.

A lot can be learned from Hegel, as I hope this book proves, and
one important thing among this lot is what's wrong with him. What
is wrong is the same thing that is also so damn right, so inescapably
right: his logic. One must understand it, the way he would want us
to—from the inside. *And then* one must—one *ought to*, that is—take
one's leave from it. By "playing" its enemy against it.

NOTES

Chapter One

1. As will become immediately apparent, the technical Aristotelian term for this phenomenon is "homonymy." But I will also use "equivocality" and "ambiguity" to refer to it; and I will follow the convention that things are homonymous whereas linguistic expressions are equivocal or ambiguous.

2. The Greek word translated here as "name" also covers the English word "noun." For the sake of consistency, I will use "name" throughout, but the reader should keep this (metalinguistic) equivocality (?) in mind (in addition to all the object-language ones we will be talking about). Also, I will regard this definition and related ones as implicitly extending to words that are not names (or nouns), hence I will talk in general about equivocal words—following in this Aristotle's own practice (see for example p. 9 below, where the equivocality of an adverb is in question).

3. See also *Poetics* 2331–32.

4. See *Post. An.* 155: "Thus one definition of definition is the one stated; another definition is . . ."

5. A definition is not supposed to contain the term that is being defined—explicitly or implicitly. See *Topics* 240.

6. The whole-part understanding of the meaning of a word articulated here is made explicit by Aristotle at *Physics* 315: "A name, e.g. 'circle,' means vaguely a sort of whole: its definition analyzes this into particulars."

7. "It is the possession of sensation that leads us for the first time to speak of living things as *animals*" (*On the Soul* 658). See also *Sense* 693, *On Youth* 745, 747, 748, *Parts* 1014, 1018, 1038, *Progr. of An.* 1098, *Gen. of An.* 1135, 1136, 1142–43, 1150, 1173, 1204.

8. This is not to imply that each division be a *binary* one, for such a

requirement would make the definitional process "often impracticable" (see *Parts* 1000). But it is still the case that each of several differentiae *excludes* all the others.

9. See also ibid. 235–36, 266–67. At *Soph. Ref.* 298 we are told that "refutation is a non-homonymous contradiction arrived at from certain premisses," and at ibid. 299 that, "if people never made two questions into one question, the fallacy that turns upon homonymy and ambiguity would not have come about, but either genuine refutation or none." See also ibid. 309.

An additional source of confusion is the following: people might be led to compare things to which a term applies equivocally, but "things not synonymous are all incommensurable. E.g. a pen, a wine, and the highest note in a scale are not commensurable: we cannot say whether any one of them is sharper than any other; and why is this? they are incommensurable because they are homonymous" (*Physics* 415).

10. See also *Nic. Eth.* 1782: "it follows for the most part that if one contrary is ambiguous the other also will be ambiguous; e.g. if 'just' is so, that 'unjust' will be so too."

11. For similar statements see *Parts* 1035, *Gen. of An.* 1130, *Magna Moralia* 1910, *Eud. Eth.* 1977.

12. See also ibid. 12.

13. See also ibid. 146.

14. Similar statements can be found at *Met.* 1676, 1717. At ibid. 1717–18 the complication is added that "knowledge . . . is spoken of in two ways—as potential and as actual," and consequently "the statement that all knowledge is universal . . . is in a sense true, although in a sense it is not." In due course, we will have to bring that crucial source of equivocality (?) center stage.

15. Conversely, "it is not permissible to break up a natural group" (*Parts* 1000). In this connection, see note 19 below.

16. This recurrent example is used to make the same point at ibid. 1626. When it surfaces again in the *Poetics* its comparison class is quite different— and when we get to that use of it our understanding of the situation will have gone through quite a momentous revolution.

17. See also ibid. 235, 259, *Met.* 1645.

18. "Acumen is a talent for hitting upon the middle term in an imperceptible time" (*Post. An.* 147). And "the middle term" is another name for the universal ("the middle term is the explanation," ibid. 148)—and one that will acquire major relevance when we turn to Hegel.

19. To make matters worse, there is a gradual, imperceptible transition between genuine universals and homonymies, which makes it harder to spot the latter: "some homonymies are far removed from one another, some have a certain likeness, and some are nearly related either generically or analogically, with the result that they seem not to be homonymies though they really are" (*Physics* 416). This troublesome graduality will turn out to be a blessing in the alternative, Hegelian account to be developed later.

Note also that, in escaping the threat of homonymy, we must avoid falling into the opposite extreme of separating things that essentially belong together (say, white men from nonwhite ones)—which once again would amount to a failure of carving nature at its joints. The following passage from *Parts* 1011 alerts us to this other threat: "blood is hot in *one* way; for it is spoken of as boiling water would be were it denoted by a single term. But the substratum of blood, that which it is while it is blood is not hot. Blood then in a certain sense is essentially hot, and in another sense is not so. For heat is included in the definition of blood, just as whiteness is included in the definition of a white man; but so far as blood becomes hot from some external influence, it is not hot essentially." Thus, to design a language adequate to proper scientific inquiry, we must navigate the difficult passage between the Scylla of homonymous connections and the Charibdis of accidental ones. ("We must . . . say regarding the *accidental*, that there can be no scientific treatment of it," *Met.* 1620–21; see also ibid. 1622, 1682.) Both dangers are serious, but here I focus on the one that is more relevant to my present concerns.

20. See ibid. 318, 351, *On the Soul* 653, 657, *Met.* 1620, 1623, 1646, 1651, 1660, 1664–65.

21. See also *Physics* 380.

22. See also *Topics* 213–14, *Met.* 1577, 1664.

23. "A picture painted on a panel is at once a picture and a likeness: that is, while one and the same, it is both of these, although the being of both is not the same, and one may contemplate it either as a picture, or as a likeness. Just in the same way we have to conceive that the image within us is both something in itself and relative to something else. Insofar as it is regarded in itself, it is only an object of contemplation, or an image; but when considered as relative to something else, e.g., as its likeness, it is also a reminder" (*On Memory* 716).

24. Note that this strategy only applies to cases in which "the same" word has a finite number of (distinct) meanings—we are back at facing the fact that we can only count on finite linguistic resources. What might seem here a bothersome empirical constraint will reveal fundamental conceptual implications when we turn to Hegel.

25. That this indeed be the case with "sharp," incidentally, is suggested by Aristotle himself: "A sharp angle is one that is less than a right angle, while a sharp dagger is one cut at a sharp angle" (*Topics* 178). "Sharp and flat are here [that is, in the realm of sounds] metaphors, transferred from their proper sphere, viz. that of touch. . . . There seems to be a sort of parallelism between what is sharp or flat to hearing and what is sharp or blunt to touch" (*On the Soul* 669).

26. See also ibid. 1623, 1626–27.

27. The same point is made at ibid. 609, 611.

28. Other examples of extension of meaning can be found at *Nic. Eth.* 1813–14, *Eud. Eth.* 1949.

29. Thus, semantic drift is what is responsible for the ubiquitousness of homonymy. That homonymy be *possible* is due, as we have seen, to our

necessity of gathering things and to the constant risk of doing it "the wrong way." But that *in fact* we go wrong so often is due to meanings changing all the time.

30. The same example occurs at *Rhetoric* 2162.

31. See for example *Hist. of An.* 924: "In the case of all these animals [intermediate between terrestrial and aquatic] their nature appears in some kind of a way to have got warped." Also, molluscs, which "are moving if regarded as sedentary creatures . . . , sedentary if classed with progressing animals," "we must . . . treat all . . . as mutilated" and indeed as moving "in a manner contrary to nature" (*Progr. of An.* 1109; see also note 4 of Chapter 3). (A curiosity: "mutilated" is the only term, of all those treated in Book V of the *Metaphysics*, that does not have multiple meanings [see 1617].)

32. The discussion above should suggest the main direction such fixing will take (one indeed to which we have seen Aristotle himself to be inclined at times). It will amount to introducing technical terms that can be arbitrarily defined, hence whose meanings can be assigned whatever structure we consider serviceable. This tactic in turn will generate the problem of eventually relating technical terms and their meanings to the natural language where we conduct our ordinary business—a language about which, for obvious reasons, one will often pass dismissive and derogatory judgments. We will see that Hegel, on the other hand, shows great respect for natural language.

Chapter Two

1. See also *Aesthetics* 128–29: " 'Sense' is this wonderful word which is used in two opposite meanings. On the one hand it means the organ of immediate apprehension, but on the other hand we mean by it the sense, the significance, the thought, the universal underlying the thing."

2. As we turn to the task of examining the contrast between Aristotle and Hegel (which, as we will see, includes examining Hegel's creative utilization of seminal Aristotelian suggestions), it might be instructive to cite some other enthusiastic judgments on Hegel's part about his predecessor and "antagonist." All of the following quotes are from *Philosophy* II: "[Aristotle] was one of the richest and deepest of all the scientific geniuses that have as yet appeared—a man whose like no later age has ever yet produced" (117). "Aristotle excels Plato in speculative depth, for he was acquainted with the deepest kind of speculation—idealism" (119). "If we would be serious with philosophy, nothing would be more desirable than to lecture upon Aristotle, for he is of all the ancients the most deserving of study" (134). "Aristotle is so rich a treasure-house of philosophic conceptions, that much material is found in him which is ready for further working upon" (224).

3. The approach in terms of essence is contained in Book VII of the *Metaphysics;* the one in terms of potentiality and actuality is in Book IX.

4. See also *Met.* 1720: "the matter of each thing . . . must be that which

is potentially of the nature in question. . . . Everything comes to be what it comes to be out of that which is it potentially."

5. See also *Physics* 330: "a thing is more properly said to be what it is when it exists in actuality than when it exists potentially." In addition to the homonymy that might exist between being-potentially and being-actually, homonymies threaten (as indeed was suggested in the quote above from *Met.* 1657) within those two terms themselves: "The term 'potentially' is used in more than one way. . . . One who is learning a science knows potentially in a different way from one who while already possessing the knowledge is not actually exercising it" (*Physics* 426). "We must now distinguish different senses in which things can be said to be potential or actual" (*On the Soul* 664). " 'Potentiality' and the word 'can' have several senses. Of these we may neglect all the potentialities that are so called homonymously" (*Met.* 1651). And the strategy for dealing with some of these multiple senses is, once again, focal meaning: "all potentialities that conform to the same type are starting points, and are called potentialities in reference to one primary kind" (ibid.).

6. What follows is meant to have only heuristic value and to be no exegesis of Wittgenstein. For my present purposes, I am happy if there is only a "family resemblance" between what I say and a "proper" interpretation of the relevant passages of the *Philosophical Investigations*. But, of course, I find it highly instructive that such a resemblance exist: it is one more case of the kind of "return of the repressed Hegel" I mentioned in the introduction and will discuss again in Chapter 5.

7. I must hasten to guard the reader against two possible misunderstandings of this statement. First, I am not saying that a word's etymology determines (in any straightforward causal sense) the way the word is currently used and understood. On the contrary, we will see that the development of meaning is a creative one; hence one that, though it should make perfectly good sense after the fact, is bound to constantly surprise us as it happens. Second, as I proceed immediately hereafter to refine my "approximation," it will become clear that what is at issue here is not the *factual* history/etymology of a word, but its *rational* one.

8. See also *Phenomenology* 64: "It is clear that the dialectic of sense-certainty is nothing else but the simple history of its movement or of its experience, and sense-certainty itself is nothing else but just this history."

9. We will see later that the plural here is not exactly right—though it's not exactly wrong either.

10. "Philosophy fights against . . . [the] 'also' " (*Nature* 34).

11. Indeed, when it is not so redeemed, history is a villain here (and the word "history" is used to imply that something is amiss). See for example *Science* 49, 54, 59; *Right* 29. (When one of these quotes surfaces again, in Chapter 4, we will be ready to draw some devastating consequences from it— to see that not just conventional history but also conventional text and time are to be overcome.)

12. It is important to notice that the contradictions through which the meaning of a word develops have more than just theoretical significance: they signal that there is violence associated with that development. "Thus, in Roman law, for example, no definition of a *human being* would be possible, for the slave could not be subsumed under it; indeed, the status of the slave does violence to that concept. The definitions of 'property' and 'proprietor' would seem equally hazardous in many situations" (*Right* 27). That the slave contradicts the Roman understanding of "human" (the phase then reached by the meaning of that word) is not something that can be peacefully resolved by finding some new word: what is at stake is the appropriation of the very word "human"—with all of its "thickness," all of its already developed meaning—by a new constituency; and such appropriation will require the shedding of blood.

13. This enthusiastic judgment will be importantly qualified below (beginning with note 20 and the attending text). For the moment, note that the judgment is not to be taken as applying equally to all languages: some of them definitely are, according to Hegel, better expressions of spirit than others. Specifically, alphabetic written language is a vast improvement over its hieroglyphic ancestor (*Mind* 215–18) and had a highly valuable impact on vocal language, and even on spiritual life: "The progress of the vocal language depends most closely on the habit of alphabetic writing; by means of which only does vocal language acquire the precision and purity of its articulation" (ibid. 216). "[L]earning to read and write an alphabetic character . . . leads the spirit from the sensibly concrete image to attend to the more formal structure of the vocal word and its abstract elements, and contributes much to give stability and independence to the inward realm of the subject" (ibid. 218; translation modified).

14. Similarly, a reformulation of his philosophy in linguistic terms would have the effect of transfiguring our ordinary understanding of language. See note 22 of Chapter 4 and the attending text.

15. See also *Aesthetics* 167: "the word is the product of our ideas, and therefore carries in itself the character of the universal." The delusive sense of being able to make contact with individuals through demonstratives like "this" and "that" (see, for example, *Phenomenology* 58ff) will become the focus of attention later.

16. There is more to this passage—specifically, the reference to the idea—than can be explained here. Any account of Hegel must be conceived and used in the way Hegel himself indicates: one must enter it at some largely arbitrary point, where lots of things look quite mysterious, and then gradually redeem this arbitrariness by returning to the beginning after the "end" was reached, in a circular movement that will eventually overcome the very notion that there is any "beginning" to it. (I will return to this circularity in Chapters 3 and 4; and in note 18 of Chapter 4 I will take a more understanding, retrospective look at the Hegelian nature of my methodology.)

17. "The procedure of the older metaphysics . . . did not go beyond the

thinking of mere *understanding*. . . . When we are discussing thinking we must distinguish *finite* thinking, the thinking of the mere *understanding*, from the *infinite* thinking of *reason*. Taken in isolation, just as they are immediately given, the thought-determinations are *finite* determinations" (*Logic* 66; the terms "finite" and "infinite" will be clarified shortly). "It is only the ordinary abstract understanding that takes the determinations of immediacy and mediation to be absolute, each on its own account, and thinks that it has an example of a *firm* distinction in them; in this way, it engenders for itself the unsurmountable difficulty of uniting them" (ibid. 118).

18. As Hegel phrases the contrast at *Religion* II 573, "allness is initially represented in such a way that the singular things remain independent. But the universality of thinking, substantial universality, is a unity with itself in which everything singular or particular is only something ideal, and has no true being."

19. See, for example, the section On the Amphiboly of Concepts of Reflection in the first *Critique* (A260ff B316ff).

20. For it is, after all, only the "*external* manifestation" of "theoretic intelligence" (*History* 63), or "an *outer* reality that is immediately self-conscious existence" (*Phenomenology* 430; italics mine), or "a self-manifestation of spirit *in externality*" (*Aesthetics* 701; italics mine; in the original German of these three quotes, the reference is always to "die Sprache," though the last one also refers in the same breath to "die Rede"; in the English, "die Sprache" is translated as "speech" in the first quote and as "language" in the other two, and "die Rede" is translated as "speech"), or the "most malleable *material*, the direct *property* of the spirit" (ibid. 972; italics mine)—and that is why it "attains . . . a high intellectual development" even "prior to the commencement of civilization" (*History* 69). So, whereas "what is ineffable is, in truth, only something obscure, fermenting, something which gains clarity only when it is able to put itself into words," and hence "the word gives to thoughts their highest and truest existence" (*Mind* 221), we should be able to overcome this external existence if we are to use language properly. I explore the details and consequences of such overcoming in Chapter 4.

21. This "general standpoint" must not entail that contingency is entirely eliminated from the world: a (significant) role must still be found for it. Hegel faced this issue early (in *Krug*) and, as noted by H. Harris (in his introduction to the translation of that essay), the challenge posed by Wilhelm Krug (that transcendental idealism should be able to "deduce" his pen) "stuck in Hegel's mind" and continued to function "as the irritant that forced him to deal with this problem" (293). Krug in fact will be mentioned again in *Nature* 23n; as far as the present book is concerned, I will address the issue in Chapter 4.

22. The qualification is crucial, since it is identity *in difference* that we are talking about.

23. A similar passage occurs at *Logic* 154.

24. The most extreme Hegelian formulations of the (highly controversial) attitude to which this is a reaction can be found in his philosophy of nature,

starting with his dissertation *On the Orbits of Planets*, where we read statements like the following: "I will prove what value philosophy has even in determining the mathematical relations among magnitudes" (237; my translation). "The ratios among the distances of planets . . . seem to pertain only to experience. In truth, measure and number in nature cannot be foreign to reason" (252; my translation). See also *Nature* 80: "It may seem strange to want to fit the comets into this system; but what exists must necessarily be embraced by the concept." And *Mind* 77: "why we have just the familiar *five* senses, no more and no less, with their distinctive forms, the rational necessity of this must, in a philosophical treatment, be demonstrated."

25. At times, Hegel himself brings out this distinction; for example, at *Logic* 236–37, where he says that "the concept can . . . be called abstract, . . . if we understand by 'concrete' what is sensibly concrete, and in general what is immediately perceptible; for the concept as such will not let us grasp it with our hands, and, in general, when the concept is in question, hearing and seeing are things of the past. All the same, . . . the concept is also what is utterly concrete, precisely because it contains being and essence, and hence all the riches of both these spheres, within itself in ideal unity"; and at *Philosophy* I 40, where he says that "we must . . . distinguish the naturally concrete from the concrete of thought, which on its side, again, is wanting in sensuous matter." But, of course, this is not *just* a distinction: it will eventually be superseded. So, in the context of the last quote, he adds: "Feeling and sense-perception come first, thought last, and thus feeling *appears* to us to be more concrete than thought, or the activity of abstraction and of the universal. *In reality, it is just the other way*" (italics mine).

26. See also *Religion* III 71: "the concept [in our sense] is not what is ordinarily meant by 'concept,' i.e., something opposed to objective reality, something that is *not supposed* to have being in it."

27. Which includes resisting the very distinction between understanding and reason: "the usual practice of separating understanding and reason is, from every point of view, to be rejected" (*Science* 612). Just as with traditional concepts—with the traditional concept of concept—understanding too must not be sidelined, but appropriated. In Chapter 5 I will discuss the general significance of this argumentative strategy.

28. And you would be just as unsympathetic to the practice followed by your own translators of making your ordinary words appear new—specifically, of rendering your ordinary word "Begriff" as "Notion," or as a capitalized "Concept" to be neatly contrasted with its run-of-the-mill, lowercase cousin.

29. At this stage, I am using "spirit" and "concept" as virtual synonyms. It will take a while before I can bring out what richer content the former expresses. Also, note that "life," too, will undergo a similar maturation and clarification as it extends to concept and spirit: "the power of life, and still more the might of the spirit, consists precisely in positing contradiction in itself, enduring it, and overcoming it. This positing and resolving of the contradiction between the ideal unity and the real separateness of the members

constitutes the constant process of life, and life *is* only by being a *process*" (*Aesthetics* 120).

30. At *Nature* 274, Hegel says that absolute idealism is "the perpetual action of life." And at ibid. 352 he says that "the life of the animal . . . is . . . the absolute idealism of possessing within itself the determinateness of its bodily nature in a perfectly fluid form."

31. "The idea is essentially *process*, because its identity is only the absolute and free identity of the concept, because this identity is the absolute negativity and hence dialectical" (*Logic* 290). More specifically, "the subjective element of thought and . . . [the] objective content are really in their diversity the passing into one another, and . . . this identity is their truth" (*Philosophy* II 317).

32. The qualifications "only" and "also" are needed because the opposition between substance and subject is not to be thought of as radical either—it too will have to be conquered by the universal narrative.

33. See also *Religion* II 622: "The unifying within self of opposed principles is what subjectivity is—it is the might to endure and resolve this contradiction within itself. . . . A subject is this distinction, something inwardly concrete, a development in which subjectivity introduces itself into the developed powers and unites them in such a way that this subject has a history, the history of life and of spirit. It is inner movement, in which it fragments into the distinction of these powers and inverts itself into something strange to itself."

34. Some phases of this dynamics manifest its turmoil better than others. Thus, "*becoming* is the true expression of the result of being and nothing; it is not just the *unity* of being and nothing, but it is inward *unrest*—a unity which in its self-relation is not simply motionless, but which, in virtue of the diversity of being and nothing which it contains, is inwardly turned against itself.—*Being-there*, on the contrary, is this *unity* or becoming in this form of unity; that is why it is *one-sided* and *finite*" (*Logic* 143). But any such finite resting point will be overcome in the *universal* unrest.

35. In the First Analogy of Experience in the first *Critique*, A182ff B224ff.

36. He indeed claims that "we must not be so tender toward matter. It is only in the understanding's 'system of identity' that matter perdures" (*Nature* 109).

37. "It may certainly be the case with a single nation that its culture, art, science—its intellectual activities as a whole—are at a standstill" (*Philosophy* I 3).

38. Essentially the same point is made at *Science* 117.

39. See also *Nature* 13, *Religion* II 93. There is another major use of the word "truth" in Hegel, consistent with the one articulated here. It occurs in the expression "the truth of" (see for example *Science* 512, *Mind* 8, 30, *Right* 186, *Religion* I 464, *Religion* II 191, 382), as when we say that the truth of a promise is its later fulfillment (if it is fulfilled), or the truth of a seed is the plant that grows from it (if one does); what the expression in general refers

to is some later phase in the development of something, in which "its concept" (that is, what it implicitly was all along) manifests itself more clearly.
And of course, in doing this, the thing (the content) is also brought into
clearer harmony with itself.

40. Since this last thesis entails the previous two, Hegel is of course also
committed to them.

41. I explore this line of argument in detail in Chapter 6 of my *Kant's
Copernican Revolution*.

42. "The right form is so far from being indifferent with respect to content
. . . that, on the contrary, it is the content itself" (*Logic* 202–3). "In spirit, . . .
form and content are identical with each other" (*Mind* 17).

43. Or, as Hegel himself would put it, "each of the parts of philosophy
is a philosophical whole, a circle that closes upon itself" (*Logic* 39).

44. It is suggestive to pursue the analogy with chaos theory a little further.
On the one hand, (unpredictable, nonlinear) meteorological phenomena were
a major impetus for this theory. On the other hand, Hegel reverses the
centuries-old (and, specifically, Aristotelian) valorization of the supralunar
world over the sublunar one. "The stars can be admired on account of their
repose, but they are not to be reckoned as equal in dignity to the concrete
individual bodies" (*Nature* 62). Indeed, they are "as little worthy of wonder-
ment as an eruption on the skin or a swarm of flies" (ibid.). "If there is a
question of pride of place, we must give the place of honor to the earth we
live on" (ibid. 104) because individuality is manifested there more than anywhere else. Specifically, "the individual identity which binds together the
different elements, as well as their difference from one another and from their
unity, is a dialectic which constitutes the physical life of the earth, the *meteorological process*" (ibid. 113). So, the supreme regularity of the starry heaven,
which the tradition regarded with awe, Hegel finds tedious; but meteorological phenomena he regards with interest. (And, when such phenomena are
treated with the traditional categories of the understanding, "each physical
existence becomes . . . *chaos*," *Nature* 114. As indeed in chaos theory, there is
no chaos in nature—only more complexity than we [or the understanding in
us] might have liked.) See also *Aesthetics* 139, where the oval is regarded as
expressing "higher freedom" and "inner conformity to law" than circles, el-
lipses, or parabolas because "it conforms to law, but it has not been possible
to discover the law and to calculate it mathematically."

45. "The critical philosophy had . . . already turned metaphysics into
logic" (*Science* 51).

46. Needless to say, this statement holds for Hegel only if logic is taken
in *his* (dialectical) sense. Any attempt at founding philosophy on traditional
logic, however, or at reducing the former to the latter, would be seriously
misguided. See, for example, Hegel's excoriating criticism of such an attempt
by Reinhold in *Difference* 179ff: "The founding and grounding tendency . . . ,
with all the crowded press of its corroborations and analyses, its becauses and
insofars, its therefores and ifs neither gets out of itself nor into philosophy.

. . . But the founding-hunt is always busy searching for the handle, and making the run-up for living philosophy. Making the run-up becomes its true work; its very principle makes it impossible for it to arrive at knowledge and philosophy." Which brings out a radical difference between the attitudes of Kant and Hegel in this regard: however *in fact* revolutionary Kant's logic might be, he famously thinks of this discipline as having been since Aristotle "not . . . able to advance a single step, and hence . . . [as being] to all appearances closed and completed" (*Critique of Pure Reason* Bviii). Hegel, on the other hand, is perfectly self-conscious about the import of his revolutionary practice, and that is why he can say that "psychology, like logic, is one of those sciences which in modern times have yet derived least profit from the more general mental culture and the deeper conception of reason. It is still extremely ill off" (*Mind* 186).

47. As I argue in *Kant's Copernican Revolution*, this is how Kant's response to Hume's skepticism must be understood: not as a(n attempted) refutation of it, but as an articulation of what kind of philosophy can (and must) be done in the wake of it. I make similar points about the philosophy of language and about ethics in "A New Paradigm of Meaning" and "Taking Care of Ethical Relativism."

48. See note 20 of Chapter 5 and the attending text. When we do get to that stage, incidentally, we will see yet another (related) example of building on a problem as opposed to trying to make it vanish: the strategy I recommend there for handling the danger presented by dialectical logic is to be found in moving beyond it, not away from it.

Chapter Three

1. So, quite appropriately, Hegel raises the stakes for what is to be a satisfactory logical account (or, more in line with the interpretation developed here, brings to the surface the implicitly higher stakes already present in Aristotle): "In the customary treatment of logic hitherto, various *classifications* and *species* of concepts occur. We are at once struck by the inconsequential way in which the species of concepts are introduced: *there are*, in respect of quantity, quality, etc., the following concepts. *There are*, expresses no other justification than that we *find* such species *already to hand* and they present themselves *empirically*. In this way, we obtain an *empirical logic*—an odd science this, an *irrational* cognition of the *rational*. In proceeding thus, logic sets a very bad example of obedience to its own precepts; it permits itself for its own purpose to do the opposite of what it prescribes as a rule, namely that concepts should be deduced, and scientific propositions (therefore also the proposition: there are such and such species of concepts) should be proved" (*Science* 613).

2. "History seems at first to be a succession of chance events, in which each fact stands isolated by itself, which has time alone as a connecting link. But even in political history we are not satisfied with this. We see, or at least divine in it, that essential connection in which the individual events have

their place and relation to an end or aim, and in this way obtain significance" (*Philosophy* I 6). "From every history a moral may be extracted" (*Religion* I 400). But see note 11 in Chapter 2 and the references made there.

3. At times Aristotle suggests that this episodic character may be bad for scientific, non-fictional stories, too: "those who . . . generate one kind of substance after another and give different principles for each, make the substance of the universe a series of episodes . . . , and they give us many principles; but the world must not be governed badly. 'The rule of many is not good; let there be one ruler' " (*Met.* 1700). "The phenomena show that nature is not a series of episodes, like a bad tragedy" (ibid. 1723).

4. An interesting wrinkle is added at 2339, where Aristotle says that "there is no possible apology for improbability or depravity [whereas there is, importantly, for contradictions], *when they are not necessary and no use is made of them*" (italics mine). The main reason for the qualifications is that sometimes a second-order probability is in play: "there is a probability of things happening also against probability" (ibid.—see also *Rhetoric* 2235: "what is improbable does happen, and therefore it is probable that improbable things *will* happen"). And such second-order probability can be used to generate second-order characterizations, as indeed is the case for inconsistency: "even if inconsistency be part of the man before one for imitation as presenting that form of character, he should still be consistently inconsistent" (2327).

Similarly, Aristotle claims both that "nature makes nothing contrary to nature" (*Progr. of An.* 1105) and that "in the realm of nature occurrences take place which are even contrary to nature" (*On Memory* 719). The reason is that "nothing can happen contrary to nature considered as eternal and necessary, but only in those cases where things generally happen in a certain way but may also happen in another way," hence in the end "even that which is contrary to nature is in a certain sense according to nature, whenever, that is, the formal nature has not mastered the material nature" (*Gen. of An.* 1192; see also ibid. 1202). In other words, since (we know already) "it is that which happens as a regular thing that is according to nature" (ibid. 1130), it regularly occurs that irregular things occur—because of how incompletely mastered matter is. (In Chapter 4, we will see that Hegel agrees on this incomplete mastery and on its consequences.)

5. See also *Met.* 1617.

6. Some such decisions, to be sure, are definitely better than others: "The *ground*, the *reason*, why the beginning is made with pure being in the pure science [of logic] is directly given in the science itself. . . . It lies in the *very nature of a beginning* that it must be being and nothing else. To enter into philosophy, therefore, calls for no other preparations, no further reflections or points of connection" (*Science* 72). "The beginning is always constituted by what is abstract and indeterminate in its meaning" (*Aesthetics* 317). But see also note 11 below.

7. See *Aesthetics* 527: "the heart . . . bends back the otherwise rectilinea

repetition of birth, death, and rebirth into the true rotation . . . and into the genuine phoenix-life of the spirit."

8. This way of reading the corpus would imply that Aristotle's "logic" is just as extensive as Hegel's—only not as self-consciously so (indeed, even in contradiction with some of his explicit pronouncements—say, the one at *De Int.* 26 where logic is radically opposed to rhetoric and poetry). That is, it would imply that all of Aristotle's "substantive" works *also* (only?) contain an implicit articulation of his logical ones; and that to account for Aristotle's logic one has to pay as much (or more) attention to his logical practice as (than) to his specific theorization of logic. Such implications are endorsed by Hegel: after claiming that Aristotle's logic is but "a natural history of finite thought" (*Philosophy* II 211), he goes on to add that, "in his metaphysics, physics, psychology, etc., Aristotle has not formed conclusions, but thought the concept in and for itself" (ibid. 217), and that "it must not be thought that it is in accordance with . . . syllogisms that Aristotle has thought. If Aristotle did so, he would not be the speculative philosopher that we have recognized him to be" (ibid. 223). Hence, Hegel concludes (consistently with my suggestion in the text), "like the whole of Aristotle's philosophy, his logic really requires recasting, so that all his determinations should be brought into a necessary systematic whole" (ibid.).

9. Hegel, by the way, agrees with Aristotle on what makes for a good story: "Action and event, taken in the stricter sense of the ideal and classical art, require an inherently true and absolutely necessary end; such an end includes in itself what determines both its external shape and also the manner of carrying it out in the real world" (*Aesthetics* 587). The term of comparison for "stricter" in this passage is romantic art, where "the specific character and complication . . . [of an adventure] are determined from without and accidentally, and so lead to accidental collisions as the extraordinarily intertwined ramifications of the situation" (ibid.); and that is one main reason why romantic art represents the (long) agony of art as such (for remember: "at first art only *seeks* its adequate content, then *finds* it, and finally *transcends* it," ibid. 967, so that "art . . . is and remains for us a thing of the past," ibid. 11). See also ibid. 221: "collisions may be introduced in the most varied ways; but the necessity of the reaction must not be occasioned at all by something bizarre or repugnant, but by something rational and justified in itself."

10. "What is to be resolved in a denouement must previously have been unfolded in a plot and prepared in advance" (*Aesthetics* 602).

11. A distinction (which will become relevant later) should be made between this ideal, universal, circular story and the empirical, and obviously faulty, writings (or lectures) of Hegel's attempting to tell it. And one point we are already in a position to appreciate, concerning this distinction, is how awkward Hegel must have felt when forced to begin his (empirical) telling somewhere. So we are not surprised by the inordinate amount of front material his texts often contain (there has to be a beginning before the beginning,

and before that . . .), or by such statements as the following: "All that is present [at the beginning] is simply the resolve, which can also be regarded as arbitrary, that we propose to consider thought as such" (*Science* 70). "Just as a provisional, or a general, notion of a philosophy cannot be given, because only the *whole* of the science is the presentation of the idea, so the *division* of it, too, can be comprehended only from the whole presentation; [at this point] the division is only something anticipated, like the [coming] presentation from which it has to be taken" (*Logic* 42).

12. See also the following: "The concept . . . is the substance of the thing, like the seed from which the whole tree unfolds. The seed contains all of its characteristics, the entire nature of the tree: the type of its sap, the pattern of its branches, etc. However, these are not preformed, so that if one took a microscope one would see the twigs and leaves in miniature, but they are instead enveloped in a spiritual manner" (*Religion* I 175). "It belongs to the nature of the concept, its vitality and becoming, in fact its spirituality, that it does not exist at the beginning, full-grown on its own account" (*Religion* II 94). "[Spirit] involves . . . an energy enabling it to realize itself; to make itself *actually* that which it is *potentially*. According to this abstract definition it may be said of universal history, that it is the exhibition of spirit in the process of working out the knowledge of that which it is potentially. And as the germ bears in itself the whole nature of the tree, and the taste and form of its fruits, so do the first traces of spirit virtually contain the whole of that history" (*History* 17–18). "Spirit begins with a germ of infinite possibility, but *only* possibility—containing its substantial existence in an undeveloped form, as the object and goal which it reaches only in its resultant—full reality. In actual existence progress appears as an advancing from the imperfect to the more perfect; but the former must not be understood abstractly as *only* the imperfect, but as something which involves the very opposite of itself—the so-called perfect—as a *germ* or impulse" (ibid. 57). See also *Philosophy* I 22–23.

13. Which amounts to appropriating it: "In cognition, what has to be done is all a matter of stripping away the alien character of the objective world that confronts us" (ibid. 273). And that, incidentally, is what *thinking* is all about: "spirit is entitled to *think* its perceptions, i.e., to raise them from their contingency to universality" (*Religion* II 750). Note also that (as indeed was suggested by the expression "stripping away" in the above quote from the *Logic*) such thinking/appropriating typically amounts to purifying matters from extraneous and irrelevant detail: "Reality is overburdened with appearance as such, with accidental and incidental things, so that often we cannot see the wood for the trees and often the greatest matter slips past us like an ordinary daily occurrence. . . . A genuinely historical portrayal . . . does not accept what is purely external and reveals only that in which the inner spirit is vividly unfolded" (*Aesthetics* 866). (This point brings up again the issue of how far contingency is still allowed within Hegel's view—an issue that I will confront systematically in Chapter 4.)

14. The narrative character of this account is what allows Hegel to claim

at the same time that aberrations are not to be taken seriously for (synchronic) classification purposes and that they are highly instructive to signal where the story is going next. A passage where this ambivalent (but dialectically consistent) attitude is given clear expression can be found at *Aesthetics* 382: "hybrid transitional stages will not fit into . . . [differentiations which are truly adequate to the concept] because they are just merely defective forms which leave one chief stage without being able to attain the following one. This is not the fault of the concept; and if we wished to take, as the basis of division and classification, such hybrids instead of the moments of the concept of the thing at issue, then what is precisely inadequate to the concept would be regarded as the adequate mode of its development. The true classification, however, may proceed only out of the true concept, and hybrid productions can only find their place where the proper explicitly stable forms begin to dissolve and pass over into others." See also ibid. 628.

15. And Aristotle might not have found it totally alien either. For remember: he characterized the poet's function as that of describing "*what is possible* as being probable and *necessary*" (see p. 45 above; italics mine).

16. In a more specific case, "the business of philosophy consists only in bringing into consciousness explicitly what people have held to be valid about thought from time immemorial. Thus, philosophy establishes nothing new; what we have brought forth by our reflection here is what everyone already takes for granted without reflection" (*Logic* 55).

17. In other passages, Hegel introduces important qualifications concerning the extent to which we can expect this project to be successful. I will turn to them in Chapter 4.

18. "Memory automatically succeeds in clothing characters, events, and actions in the garment of universality, whereby the particular external and accidental details are obscured" (*Aesthetics* 189).

19. "The past is *sublated being*, and spirit is the inward reflection of the past" (*Logic* 195).

20. See also *History* 11: "We must clearly distinguish . . . [reason from spirit]. The movement of the solar system takes place according to unchangeable laws. These laws are reason, implicit in the phenomena in question. But neither the sun nor the planets, which revolve around it according to these laws, can be said to have any consciousness of them."

21. The (most often impeccable) editor of this text finds it appropriate to add "the awareness" after "consciousness is" in this passage. I judge the gloss unjustified and misleading, and what follows in my text should explain why. See also *Mind* 164: "consciousness as such implies the reciprocal independence of subject and object." And *Religion* I 278: "Consciousness means in general [that] I am not what the object is, and the object is not what I am. Each is the other of the other, but in a determinate fashion. Each is only the negative." *Religion* III 263 introduces an interesting connection with finitude: "Consciousness is precisely the mode of finitude of spirit: distinction is present here. One thing is on one side, another on the other side; something has its

limit or end in something else, and in this way they are limited. Finitude is this distinguishing, which in spirit takes the form of consciousness."

22. In *Philosophy* III 46, Hegel says the following of spirit (of which, as I said, I will treat explicitly in the next section): "Spirit is the making for itself a pre-supposition, the giving to itself the natural as a counterpoise, the separating itself therefrom, thus the making it an object, and then for the first time the working upon this hypothesis, formulating it, and from itself bringing it forth, begetting it, internally reconstructing it."

23. Part of what I am doing in this section and the next one is unpacking Hegel's use of expressions like "in itself," "for us," and "for itself."

24. See also *Religion* II 514n: "the concept is, as it were, a potentiality within spirit, it constitutes the innermost truth, but spirit must attain to the knowledge of this truth."

25. "*Externality* constitutes the specific character in which nature, as nature, exists" (*Nature* 14). "It is characteristic of nature to do just this, to let an abstract, separate moment exist independently" (ibid. 61). "Nature is . . . the idea in the element of asunderness" (ibid. 163). "Nature is the idea implicitly and *only* implicitly, and the mode of its existence is *to be outside itself* in complete externality" (*Religion* I 227n).

26. "Spirit is no less *before* than *after* nature, it is not merely the metaphysical idea of it. Spirit, just because it is the goal of nature, is *prior* to it, nature has proceeded from spirit: not empirically, however, but in such a manner that spirit is already from the very first implicitly present in nature which is spirit's own presupposition" (*Nature* 444).

27. "Itself is its own object of attainment, and the sole aim of spirit" (*History* 19). "Spirit is . . . in its every act only apprehending itself, and the aim of all genuine science is just this, that spirit shall recognize itself in everything in heaven and on earth. An out-and-out other simply does not exist for spirit" (*Mind* 1). "Spirit is just this: to be for itself, to be for spirit" (*Religion* I 139).

28. The reverse is true as well: "only spirit can [re]cognize spirit" (*Logic* 47); "spirit reveals itself only to spirit" (*Religion* I 339).

29. There is complete continuity, hence dialectical identity in difference, between the teleological behavioral structures displayed by animals and the emergence of explicitly conscious purposefulness in humans: "The difficulty [in understanding instinct] comes mainly from representing the *teleological* relationship as *external*, and from the prevalent opinion that an *end* exists *only* in *consciousness*. Instinct is purposive activity acting unconsciously" (*Nature* 389).

30. Though the difference is still there and prevents total, indiscriminate identification: "We can understand a dog without being able to share its sensations" (*Religion* II 271). "To put oneself in the place of a dog requires the sensibilities of a dog. We are cognizant of the nature of such living objects, but we cannot possibly know what it would mean to transpose ourselves into their place, so that we could sense their determinate limits; for that would

mean filling the totality of one's subjectivity wholly with these characteristics. They remain always objects of our thought, not of our subjectivity, of our feeling" (ibid. 536). (The contexts of both quotes make it clear that this incapacity of total identification extends not just to lower animals, but also to earlier phases of human civilization.)

31. The characterization of ethical life in the *Philosophy of Right* is also relevant here: "Ethical life is the *idea of freedom* as the living good which has its knowledge and volition in self-consciousness, and its actuality through self-conscious action" (189). "Whether the individual exists or not is a matter of indifference to objective ethical life, which alone has permanence and is the power by which the lives of individuals are governed" (190). "In this *actual self-consciousness* [which it now possesses], the substance knows itself and is thus an object of knowledge" (ibid.). "The ethical substance, as containing self-consciousness which has being for itself and is united with its concept, is the *actual spirit* of a family and a people" (197).

32. This suggestion seems to contradict Hegel's recurrent signaling out of humans—indeed, of the human body—as a privileged seat of spirit. But the privilege is limited to what can take a *sensuous* shape ("if a manifestation of God is to be supposed at all, his natural form must be that of spirit, which for sensuous conception is essentially the human; for no other form can lay claim to spirituality," *History* 249; see also ibid. 324, *Mind* 294, *Religion* II 310, 660n, *Aesthetics* 78, 433). And spirit develops well past its sensuous manifestations: the state—which cannot be regarded as having physical shape—must be thought of as such a later development. At *Mind* 14, we find a sentence stating that "it is only man who is thinking spirit." But the statement is an artifice of translation: the whole paragraph is concerned with the emergence of spirit from nature, and humans are being contrasted there with (other) animals: "the animal . . . represents only the non-spiritual dialectic of transition from one single sensation filling its whole soul to another single sensation which equally exclusively dominates it; it is man who first raises himself above the singleness of sensation to the universality of thought" (ibid.). And the "only" in the first quote translates the same German word as the "first" in the second one: "erst." (A clearer statement to the same effect can be found later, when Hegel says: "Seen from the animal world, the human figure is the supreme phase in which spirit makes an appearance. But for the spirit it is only its first appearance," ibid. 147.)

A different (and more serious) problem is posed by the following passages: "An epic poem as an actual work of art can spring from *one* individual only. Although an epic does express the affairs of an entire nation, it is only individuals who can write poetry, a nation collectively cannot. . . . For poetry is a spiritual production, and the spirit exists only as an actual individual consciousness and self-consciousness" (*Aesthetics* 1049). "The personality of the state has actuality only as a *person*, as *the monarch*.—Personality expresses the concept as such, whereas the person also embodies the actuality of the concept, and only when it is determined in this way [i.e., as a person] is the concept *idea* or truth.—A so-called *moral person*, [such as] a society, community, or family, however concrete it may be in itself, contains personality only abstractly as one of its moments" (*Right* 317–18). I address this problem below and (as I say there) will return to it in Chapter 4.

33. Similarly, "the solemn declaration of consent to the ethical bond of marriage and its recognition and confirmation by the family and community constitute the formal *conclusion* and *actuality* of marriage," and it belongs to "impertinence and its ally, the understanding, which cannot grasp the speculative nature of the substantial relationship," to see "the ceremony whereby the essence of this bond is expressed and *confirmed* . . . as an *external formality*," thus presuming "to impart the highest conception of the freedom, inwardness, and perfection of love" while in fact denying its "ethical [hence, ultimately, its spiritual] character" (*Right* 204–5).

34. These two languages are, after all, but different angles on the same (spiritual) reality—as indeed are some others: "It is . . . *one individuality* which, presented in its essence as God, is honored and enjoyed in *religion*; which is exhibited as an object of sensuous contemplation in *art*; and is apprehended as an intellectual conception, in *philosophy*. In virtue of the original identity of their essence, purport, and object, these various forms are inseparably united with the spirit of the state. Only in connection with this particular religion, can this particular political constitution exist; just as in such or such a state, such or such a philosophy or order of art" (*History* 53). "Universally speaking, religion and the foundation of the state are one and the same— they are implicitly and explicitly identical" (*Religion* I 452). See also ibid. 234, *History* 335, 417, 449, *Philosophy* I 54.

35. That the two issues surfacing here (communal self-consciousness is not mental self-consciousness writ large, and individual human self-consciousness is still a necessary moment of spirit) are distinct can indeed be seen in the following way: when it surfaces, the relevant individual human self-consciousness does not necessarily have the same level of transparency (that is, of concrete detail) universal self-consciousness has. That a king be a necessity in a state, or that a poem could not come about without a(n) individual human) poet (see note 32 above), is perfectly compatible with a king or a poet having only limited understanding of what they are doing, *and* with communal practices making a much more perspicuous display of such understanding. For the specific case of the monarch, the following is a relevant passage: "A frequent objection to monarchy is that it makes the affairs of the state subject to contingency—since the monarch may be ill-educated or unworthy of holding the highest office—and that it is absurd for such a situation to be regarded as rational. But this objection is based on the invalid assumption that the monarch's particular character is of vital importance. In a fully organized state, it is only a question of the highest instance of formal decision, and all that is required in a monarch is someone to say 'yes' and to dot the 'i'; for the supreme office should be such that the particular character of its occupant is of no significance. . . . In a well-ordered monarchy, the objective

aspect is solely the concern of the law, to which the monarch merely has to add his subjective 'I will' " (*Right* 322–23).

Chapter Four

1. See also the following: "Philosophy, like empiricism, is cognizant only of what *is*; it does not know that which only *ought* to be, and for that reason *is not there*" (*Logic* 77). "The individual is the offspring of his people, of his world, whose constitution and attributes are alone manifested in his form; he may spread himself out as he will, he cannot escape out of his time any more than out of his skin" (*Philosophy* I 45). "The religion present and presupposed in everyone is the stuff that we merely want to comprehend. . . . It is not a question of bringing something substantially new and alien in humanity" (*Religion* I 89). "Every man is a child of his time in every activity, whether political, religious, or scientific" (*Aesthetics* 603). Hegel does allow for a legitimate use of "ought to" (German "soll"), but that has nothing to do with passing a judgment on reality, let alone articulating worthier alternatives to it; it only expresses reality's irresistible tendency to sublate its earlier stages in favor of later, more mature ones (which constitute "the truth of" the former). See, for example, the following: "The natural soul is not the way that it ought to be, for it ought to be free spirit; the soul becomes spirit only by sublating the natural will and appetite in general" (*Religion* II 489). "As a natural soul a human being is not spirit, is not what he ought to be, any more than God, viewed as Father, is as he ought to be" (ibid. 490). "Humanity as it is by nature is not what it ought to be; human beings ought to be what they are through spirit" (ibid. 527). "The natural spirit is essentially what spirit ought not to be or to remain" (*Religion* III 93). "Immediacy is what a human being ought *not* to be, what has to be sublated" (ibid. 202).

2. Consistently with claims to be made below, Hegel goes on to add that "a foreknowledge of *this* kind is an impossibility."

3. I will return to this point, from a different angle, at the end of this chapter, and then again in Chapter 5.

4. See *Religion* II: "The eternal nature of spirit is to die to itself, to make itself finite in natural life, but through the annihilation of its natural state it comes to itself" (453n).

5. See p. 55 above.

6. Remember that consistency is only significant here because of the universal comprehensiveness of the story: it is the latter that allows one to think of (narrative) necessity as reducing to (self-)consistency (see p. 54 above). If comprehensiveness were no longer there, consistency could provide no more status than that of an arbitrary assumption—as legitimate as any alternative one.

7. This deflationary reading allows us to make sense of Hegel's claiming, on the one hand, that "Europe is *absolutely* the end of history, Asia the beginning" (*History* 103; italics mine) and, on the other, that "America is . . .

the land of the future" (ibid. 86). This reference to America clearly intimates that history is *not* at an end, as do the following passages: "It will be for future astronomy to decide whether the path has not functions more profound than the ellipse, whether it is not perhaps an oval" (*Nature* 72). "[The] entire body of peoples [of Eastern Europe] remains excluded from our consideration, because hitherto it has not appeared as an independent element in the series of phases that reason has assumed in the world. Whether it will do so hereafter, is a question that does not concern us here" (*History* 350)—because "here" is where the rational appropriation of the given takes place, hence where we must proceed on the assumption that "the truth of time . . . [is] that the goal is not the future but the past" (*Nature* 43). Finally, that history is not at an end, and that Hegel is aware of this fact (and occasionally refers to it), will cause a serious problem to emerge later, concerning the very nature of the "story" he is telling.

8. See also *Philosophy* I 54–55: "if philosophy does not stand above its time in content, it does so in form, because, as the thought and knowledge of that which is the substantial spirit of its time, it makes that spirit its object. In as far as philosophy is in the spirit of its time, the latter is its determined content in the world, although as knowledge, philosophy is above it, since it places it in the relation of object. But this is in form alone, for philosophy really has no other content."

9. For a typical statement to this effect, see the following: "We can regard the present age as concerned with religion, with religiosity, or with piety, in which no regard is had for what is objective. . . . This standpoint has been recognized in our earlier discussion, and we have already spoken of its one-sidedness" (*Religion* III 166).

10. Indeed, shortly after the last passage quoted (and already quoted on p. 52 above), Hegel adds: "Although . . . contingency is only a one-sided moment of actuality, and must therefore not be confused with it, still as a form of the idea as a whole it does deserve its due in the world of objects. . . . We . . . have to be careful that we are not misled by the well-meant striving of rational cognition into trying to show that phenomena that have the character of contingency are necessary" (*Logic* 219). Similarly, after the quote from *Nature* on p. 44 above, Hegel continues: "Contingency certainly has its place, too, but only in unessentials." See also ibid. 283, 290.

11. See note 4 of Chapter 3.

12. Which must be compatible with these contingent elements displaying perfect rationality at a more "advanced" level (see the discussion of the second sense of contingency below): "the progression of the various stages in the advance of thought may occur with the consciousness of necessity. . . . Or else it may come about without this consciousness as does a natural and *apparently* accidental process, so that while inwardly, indeed, the concept brings about its result consistently, this consistency is not made manifest. This is so in nature; in the various stages of the development of twigs, leaves, blossom and fruit, each proceeds for itself, but the inward idea is the directing and deter-

mining force which governs the progression" (*Philosophy* I 29; italics mine). Note also that the contingency of nature sometimes occasions (what look like) simple mistakes (and again, the discussion of mistakes below is relevant to a proper appreciation of this point): "If . . . nature is perverse enough to create some people who grow pale from shame and blush from fear, science must not let such inconsistencies of nature prevent it from recognizing the opposite of these irregularities as law" (*Mind* 85). (As a law at *that* level of analysis, that is, which is compatible with such "perversions" making perfectly good sense within a more sophisticated language.)

13. Thus, "indifference" is the proper attitude toward such "externalities" as fashion: one must "hand over the contingent to the contingent," for "it is folly to set oneself against the fashion" and to fuss about it—as if it was of any significance (*Philosophy* I 201, 484). But see note 11 of Chapter 5.

14. For this whole paragraph, see *Phenomenology* 205–6.

15. Another instructive example occurs at *Religion* I 419: "In the application of . . . [a mathematical] model of demonstration to the formulation of proofs of God's existence, what appears at once is the inappropriateness of wishing to exhibit a coherence of this kind in the case of God. . . . But if we now suppose that, by pointing this out, we have shown this procedure as a whole is vacuous, then this, too, is a one-sided view—and one that directly contradicts the universal consciousness of humankind."

16. See *Phenomenology* 22: "Nor *is* there such a thing as the false."

17. It should be clear why the qualification "independent" is needed, and how it is to be understood. There will be perfectly legitimate attributions of falsity within this logic, but such attributions are not definitive of the status of what they attribute falsity to: for both the attributions and their subject matter one should eventually be looking at the whole speech act, and for both Hegel's task is to show that the whole speech act is perfectly legitimate.

18. In a less than straightforward sense, one could claim that the non-verbal "story" I am going to bring out now is indeed the "meaning" of Hegel's book(s). But that would require sublating any correlation the structure of a verbal formulation is supposed to have with the structure of its meaning. The meaning of the whole book would then be the whole of (a certain phase of) spirit; and there would be no divisions in that meaning corresponding to divisions in the book, no linearity to it corresponding to the book's linearity, no external points of view in it corresponding to the (more obviously) external comments made in the book, and so on. The meaning of language would be found in an overcoming of language itself.

We might take a moment to reflect on the dialectical nature of the process that led us here. I started out with a definite question (what is the meaning of a word?) and with a primitive, "immediate" formulation of a thesis which answers that question (a meaning is a history). Everything that followed amounted to qualifying such an answer, increasing its complexity and structure, canceling *and* preserving it; and now we have reached a point in which not only the original answer but the very question is about to be *aufgehoben*—

there is no such thing as the meaning *of a word*, really, though it was exactly right to inquire about it.

Consider what an Aristotelian, analytic procedure would have been instead: I would have started with complete, rigorous definitions of all of my key terms and with a self-sufficient set of basic axioms, and then proceeded to infer from them a number of (other) claims that were already logically contained there—though they might not have been epistemically clear. And, if at any time my question had exploded, that outcome would have reflected negatively on the inquiry itself.

19. See also *Logic* 42.

20. I have already quoted some correctives to the enthusiastic claim that language is the perfect expression of spirit (where the correction amounts less to a withdrawing of the claim than to a bringing out of the limits of *expression* in general). To them I can now add the following: "The word was presumably something hard-and-fast, yet spirit makes of it what has truth. In the same way, sensible history constitutes the point of departure for spirit. These two categories [sense and spirit] must be distinguished: the chief thing that matters is spiritual consciousness, the return of spirit into itself" (*Religion* III 229). See also *Philosophy* I 88, where, after blaming Plato for his myths and Aristotle for his similes, Hegel makes the following general pronouncement: "The difficulty of representing thoughts as thoughts always attaches to the expedient of expression in sensuous form." And *Philosophy* II 12, where we are told that "it is easy enough to hand over an external possession, but the communication of ideas requires a certain skill; there is always something esoteric in this, something more than the merely exoteric."

21. "In the realm of art . . . [the spiritual] content is not present in its infinite form . . . but is present only in immediate natural and sensuous existence. But insofar as the meaning is independent, it must in art produce its shape out of itself and have the principle of its externality in itself. It must therefore revert to the natural, but as dominant over the external which, as one side of the totality of the inner itself, exists no longer as purely natural objectivity but, without independence of its own, is only the expression of spirit. . . . This is that identification of the spiritual and the natural which is adequate to the spirit and which does not rest in the neutralization of the two opposed sides but lifts the spiritual to the higher totality where it maintains itself in its opposite, *posits the natural as ideal*, and expresses itself in and on the natural" (*Aesthetics* 431–32; italics mine).

22. It must be clear then that the "speculative proposition" is not to be understood as a(n Aristotelian) species of the genus "proposition," but as a dialectical expression of the intimate contradiction existing between "speculative" and "proposition"—which ultimately leads to an *Aufhebung* of proposition itself (and of language). This is the point that was hinted at in note 14 of Chapter 2.

23. Thus we may have to say of Hegel's philosophy what he, at the beginning of his career, said of others: "It can happen that an authentic spec-

ulation does not express itself completely in its system, or that the philosophy
of the system and the system itself do not coincide. . . . So in judging philosophical systems it is particularly important to distinguish the philosophy
from the system" (*Difference* 114). But note that it would be a cardinal mistake,
after thus appreciating the limitations of linguistic expression, to try to overcome them once and for all by appealing to some mystical, speechless "experience." The painstaking labor of going out of itself in order to eventually
recover itself (and to recognize the necessity of sublating those external vicissitudes, of looking past them) is absolutely essential to spirit; indeed, it is
what spirit is all about. "The spiritual . . . is that which *relates itself to itself* and
is *determinate*, it is *other-being* and *being-for-self*, and in this determinateness, or
in its self-externality, abides within itself. . . . It must be an *object* to itself, but
just as immediately a sublated object, reflected into itself" (*Phenomenology* 14).
I will return to this theme at the end of the chapter.

24. *Right* 20; see also *Logic* 29.

25. "If I count from a particular period such as the birth of Christ, this
epoch is again only fixed by the 'now' which is ever displaced. I am now
thirty-five years old, and now is 1805 A.D.; each period is fixed only through
the other, but the whole is undetermined" (*Philosophy* I 467).

26. At *Philosophy* I 258, speaking of Melissus, Hegel says: "Eternity is an
awkward word, for it immediately makes us think of time and mingle past
and future as an infinite length of time." But then he proceeds to explain
that what must be meant in Melissus' case is "the self-identical, supersensuous,
unchangeable, pure present, which is without any time-conception." At *Difference* 134 we are told that "the true sublation of time is a timeless present,
i.e., eternity"; and at *Faith* 106 Jacobi is chastised for finding time in Spinoza's
God, "and in the absurd form of an eternal time at that" (in the ensuing
discussion, Hegel points out the connection of this theme with the debate
concerning actual infinity: eternity understood as everlastingness reduces to
eternity understood as a constant, and constantly frustrated, resurfacing of the
finite).

27. See Chapters 6 and 7 of my *Kant's Copernican Revolution*.

28. Not just dates but numbers in general, by the way, have this character
of externality for Hegel—and numerology would then be as good a case as
phrenology of trying to get (rational) blood from turnips. Consider for example the following passage: "thought is engaged . . . [in arithmetic] in an
activity which is at the same time the extreme externalization of itself, an
activity in which it is forced to move in a realm of thoughtlessness and to
combine elements which are incapable of any necessary relationships. The
subject matter is the abstract thought of *externality* itself" (*Science* 213).

29. Some dimmer than others, of course. But it is now possible *for us*
(those who have followed the development of *this* story) to also identify
ourselves with those others who lived a similarly sacrificial experience on
(even) less transparent grounds.

30. We thus have a complete resolution of the difficulty that surfaced in

note 32 of Chapter 3 and the attending text: there must be a moment of individuality to the state or to a work of art for them to be spiritual products, and there is no real contrast (only an *ideal* one) between this moment and the communal, universal aspect they *also* have.

31. Part of what is thus timelessly understood is time itself: "Philosophy is timeless comprehension, of time too and of all things generally in their eternal mode" (*Nature* 16). It is useful to reflect on what becomes in this eternal perspective of two conclusions reached above. First, Aristotelian logic was found to have a limit in the synchronic relatedness it postulated among the various traits included in a definition (see p. 52); and now we have returned to a synchronic vision. The important difference is that this is indeed a *return*: the necessary relatedness we have been looking for can only be found beyond narrative time, not before it. Second, the temporal topology discussed on pp. 70ff must also receive a "beyond-time" formulation, since all distinction between past and present is now overcome and my present is all that (timelessly) is. Therefore, that the position I take with respect to this present be that of an imminent *future* is not to be understood chronologically now, but in purely logical terms: I am (or Hegel is) at the threshold of being— beyond everything that is and on this side of everything that isn't.

32. An important antecedent for this discussion is Kant's analysis of real possibility, for which see Chapter 1 of my *Kant's Copernican Revolution*.

33. Because I recognize the intimate resonance between these two strategies—positive proposals tending to give more bite to negative judgments, the latter tending to motivate the former—I will continue to refer to them jointly, with expressions like "normative and utopian claims."

34. See also *Philosophy* I 74: "The sins of him who lies against the Holy Spirit cannot be forgiven. That lie is the refusal to be a universal, to be holy, that is to make Christ become divided, separated."

35. If these examples seem too extreme, consider the following: "If we hold firmly to the view that the human being in and for himself is free, we thereby condemn slavery. But . . . slavery occurs in the transitional phase between natural human existence and the truly ethical condition; it occurs in a world where a wrong is still right. Hence, the wrong *is valid*, so that the position it occupies is a necessary one" (*Right* 88). (See also the quotes on p. 98 below.)

36. The original German of the italicized clause reads: "nur die Philosophie begreifen und darum rechtfertigen kann." Note that this attitude does not amount to denying evil (as is done by "those learned theologians" who can always find "a positive aspect in every action" and end up concluding "that there is in fact no such thing as an *evil man*," *Right* 175), but rather to recognizing "*the necessity of evil*" or the sense in which "good and evil are inseparable" (ibid. 168). Also (and related), the justification is only legitimate when an event is made part of the one, *universal* story. Local rationalizations (like those of the theologians above) that consist in finding some plausible

reason or other—to which equally plausible reasons could be opposed—are nothing but sophistry (*Philosophy* I 367–69).

37. Hegel himself is well aware of the perverse dialectic involved here: "it is a very false idea of Christian humility and modesty to desire through one's abjectness to attain to excellence; this confession of one's own nothingness is really inward pride and great self-conceit. But for the honor of true humility we must not remain in our misery, but raise ourselves above it by laying hold of the Divine" (*Philosophy* III 454–55).

Chapter Five

1. This semantics is more than just seductive: it is seductiveness as such. Every seducer will recognize in it the essence of his practice: taking a fingertip in your hand and gradually appropriating the whole body. At the beginning, being is aloof and indifferent; at the end, it has been insinuated and possessed. One has made it one's own.

2. A superficial look at Hegel's texts might suggest that periodization is rampant in his philosophy. But remember: "The divisions and headings of the books, sections and chapters . . . do not belong to the content and body of the science."

3. See, for example, the following: "The identity of philosophy with its history is the typical form and culminating point of the resolution of temporal into eternal history" (*The Theory of Mind as Pure Act* 215). "We do distinguish from philosophy, (1) Art; (2) Religion; (3) Science; (4) Life. . . . So, then, besides the history of philosophy, we have got, it seems, to find a place for four other kinds of history; with this proviso, however, that each of these forms of spirit, insofar as it is distinct from the philosophical, strictly has no history" (ibid. 216–17; translation modified). In making such claims, of course, Gentile was following Hegelian lines. See, for example, *Philosophy* I 29: "Philosophy is system in development; the history of philosophy is the same." Also, a similar thesis was defended by Benedetto Croce; but Croce insisted more on the identity of philosophy and history (rather than philosophy and the history of philosophy) and even opposed his own position in this regard to Hegel's.

4. A major historical example of this kind of development can be found in the fate of Frege's logicist reconstruction of arithmetic. It was enough for Russell to discover a trivial contradiction in the axiomatic base of the reconstruction for the whole project to be sidelined indefinitely (and for Frege to be forced to reemerge eventually as a "later" version of himself); and from the *ruins* of that project the "winner" in the confrontation erected his own system. The reader is invited to speculate on how differently history would have looked if some key players in this drama had adopted the Hegelian strategies described below.

5. Hegel himself would definitely favor this reading: "The triumph of

cognition is the reconciliation of the antithesis" (*Religion* I 131n). "The result of the study of philosophy is that those walls of division, which are supposed to separate absolutely, become transparent; or that when we get to the bottom of things we discover absolute agreement where we thought there was the most extreme antithesis" (ibid. 165–66). And that is precisely because "philosophy is so patient and painstaking that it carefully investigates its opponent's position" (ibid. 172n).

6. For a religious variant of this attitude, see *Religion* I 197n: "The determinate religions are not indeed *our* religion, yet they are included in ours as essential though subordinate moments. . . . Therefore in them we have to do not with what is foreign to us but *with what is our own.*"

7. So it is implicit here that a colonizing attitude can be, and often is, mutual—and that who gets to actualize it depends on who can do it more forcefully.

8. Note that establishing dialectical (in)coherence is typically more complicated than in the analytic case: the presence of a contradiction is not enough to prove incoherence, but the *possibility* of *Aufhebung* is not enough to prove coherence either. What is needed for the latter (in presence of a contradiction) is the availability of a concrete (narrative) account warranting the successful sublation.

9. Some examples might be in order. In the *Science of Logic*, the third moment of quantity is the quantitative relation or quantitative ratio, whereas in *The Encyclopaedia Logic* it is degree. In the *Science of Logic* the absolute (which corresponds to Spinoza's substance) is the first moment of actuality, but in *The Encyclopaedia Logic* there is no such category (and Spinoza's substance turns up in the relationship of substantiality, where in the previous work there was no mention of it). In the 1824 *Lectures on the Philosophy of Religion* the religion of beauty (that is, Greek religion) follows the religion of sublimity (that is, Jewish religion), whereas in the 1827 lectures the order is reversed.

10. "Religion is the mode, the type of consciousness, in which the truth is present for all men, or for all levels of education; but scientific cognition is a particular type of the consciousness of truth, and not everyone, indeed only a few men, undertake the labor of it. *The basic import is the same*, but . . . there are two tongues for that import: the tongue of feeling, of representation, and of the thinking that nests in the finite categories and one-sided abstractions of understanding, and the tongue of the concrete concept" (*Logic* 11). "Religion is for everyone. It is not philosophy, which is not for everyone. Religion is the manner or mode by which all human beings become conscious of truth for themselves" (*Religion* I 180). See also *Religion* III 188–89, 256. To some extent, art works the same way: "Works of art . . . must be immediately intelligible and enjoyable in themselves. . . . For art does not exist for a small enclosed circle of a few eminent *savants* but for the nation at large and as a whole" (*Aesthetics* 273).

11. See note 13 of Chapter 4. Comparing these two contexts makes one aware of the tension involved, and of the need to negotiate it dialectically.

That everything in the world expresses the concept must not be taken to mean that a perspicuous account of that expression could be found at every level (phrenology still threatens); hence we must look for a delicate balance between trusting that reason will eventually show up and not rushing into unwarranted vindications of our trust. Thus a story can be told (of course!) according to which Hegel was not acting against his better judgment but was indeed just right in regarding fashion as dominated by sheer contingency, as much as Barthes was perfectly justified (after the emergence of semiology) in finding a rational structure in (talk of) it.

12. The way an Aristotelian would have to look at these phenomena is as providing illustrations for predetermined conceptual specifications. And, to be sure, this illustrative mode is present in most intellectual analyses of culture. But in the best of them there is something else as well: there is real drama and development, a concept that reacts with its "material" and offers more than a predictable repetition of the identical. There the spirit is undeniably Hegelian.

13. "Observation selects . . . [intention] as the true inner; the intention is supposed to have its more or less *unessential* expression in the deed. . . . [But t]he *true being* of a man is rather his deed; in this the individual is *actual*" (*Phenomenology* 192–93). "The way a man is externally, i.e., in his actions . . . , that is how he is internally; and if he is *only* internally virtuous or moral, etc., i.e., *only* in his intentions, and dispositions, and his outward is not identical with those, then the former is as hollow and empty as the latter" (*Logic* 210). "It must be said that a person *is* what he *does*" (ibid. 211). "[A] man is nothing but the series of his acts" (ibid. 212). "What is supreme and most excellent is not, as may be supposed, the inexpressible—for if so the poet would be still far deeper than his work discloses. On the contrary, his works are the best part and the truth of the artist; what he is [in his works], that he *is*; but what remains buried in his heart, that *is* he not" (*Aesthetics* 290–91). "It is . . . a sophistical understanding, devoid of any idea, which can make a distinction whereby the *thing-in-itself*, the soul, is neither touched nor affected if the *body* is abused and the *existence* of the person is subjected to the power of another" (*Right* 79). Note that the "hermeneutics of suspicion" that is the natural counterpart of this view characterizes Hegel from the start. See, for example, his treatment of Kant, Jacobi, and Fichte in *Faith*: "These philosophers are as completely confined within eudaemonism as they are diametrically opposed to it" (62–63).

14. Indeed, it seems that this "only if" could even be strengthened to an "if and only if"—that one's "promises" consist *precisely* of what one realizes through one's behavior: "What the subject *is, is the series of its actions.* If these are a series of worthless productions, then the subjectivity of volition is likewise worthless; *and conversely, if the series of the individual's deeds are of a substantial nature, then so also is his inner will*" (*Right* 151; last italics mine).

15. In this regard, see my "Kant's Sadism."

16. For the appropriateness of the term "theodicy," see the following:

"Our mode of treating the subject is . . . a Theodicaea—a justification of the ways of God—which Leibniz attempted metaphysically, in his method, i.e., in indefinite abstract categories—so that the ill that is found in the world may be comprehended, and the thinking spirit reconciled with the fact of the existence of evil. Indeed, nowhere is such a harmonizing view more pressingly demanded than in universal history; and it can be attained only by recognizing the *positive* existence, in which that negative element is a subordinate, and vanquished nullity" (*History* 15). "That the history of the world, with all the changing scenes which its annals present, is this process of development and the realization of spirit—this is the true *Theodicaea*, the justification of God in history" (ibid. 457). See also *Philosophy* III 7, 546; *Logic* 222. And note that, in commenting on the most famous of theodicies—Leibniz's—Hegel insists that, though its intentions are right, its results are not specific enough: "In a general sense we are satisfied with the answer: 'In accordance with the wisdom of God we must accept it as a fact that the laws of nature are the best possible,' but this answer does not suffice for a definite question. What one wishes to know is the goodness of this or that particular law; and to that no answer is given" (*Philosophy* III 342).

17. An analogous progressive distancing from the main source has characterized the repeated reemergence of Hegel's "message"—from British idealism to Italian neoidealism to the various kinds of holism and coherentism that have continued to enjoy (typically limited) currency to this day.

18. I am referring to Woody Allen's *Deconstructing Harry*.

19. See my *The Discipline of Subjectivity* and *Logic and Other Nonsense*.

20. It is in the context of this dual attitude that we should address the limitations of Aristotelian logic brought out in Chapter 1—those which provided the motivation for our journey through Hegel. Dialectical logic can be very helpful in providing richer articulations of meaning, essence, actuality, and scientific practice than we find *explicit* in Aristotle's texts (though, as I indicated, such articulations can also be seen as budding there); but one must resist the temptation, after succeeding at this enterprise, to rest content with a single, all-inclusive story. For reasons that I expound below, there must still be room for analysis: for a surfacing of the partiality of *any* story. In terms of the alternatives offered on p. 20, I have (unceremoniously, and without much argument) rejected the ordinary "fixing" of the Aristotelian scheme through the introduction of technical terms, and now I have shown the danger that follows upon "trying a different tack altogether"—at least, *this* different tack. What is left is "learning to live with the shakiness"—or even loving it after we realize how enslaving stability can be: doing one's best to indeed keep the search for the proper logico/scientific correspondence between words (not just *all* words but also *each* one of them) and world an interminable one. And here is where a local use of dialectical logic can help; for, as I argue in the text, nothing reveals the partiality of a(n allegedly comprehensive) story better than the telling of another one displaying similar ambitions.

21. See the *Critique of Pure Reason*, A5 B8.

BIBLIOGRAPHY

Bencivenga, Ermanno. *The Discipline of Subjectivity*. Princeton: Princeton University Press, 1990.

———. "Free from What?" In *Looser Ends: The Practice of Philosophy*. 120–29. Minneapolis: University of Minnesota Press, 1989.

———. *Kant's Copernican Revolution*. New York: Oxford University Press, 1987.

———. "Kant's Sadism." *Philosophy and Literature* 20 (1996): 39–46.

———. *Logic and Other Nonsense*. Princeton: Princeton University Press, 1993.

———. "A New Paradigm of Meaning." In *Looser Ends*. 62–79.

———. "Taking Care of Ethical Relativism." *Philosophical Forum* 26 (1995): 288–93.

Gentile, Giovanni. *The Theory of Mind as Pure Act*. Translated by H. Carr. London: Macmillan, 1922.

Kant, Immanuel. *Critique of Pure Reason*. Translated by W. Pluhar. Indianapolis: Hackett, 1996.

———. *Religion within the Limits of Reason Alone*. Translated by T. Greene and H. Hudson. New York: Harper, 1960.

Malcolm, Norman. *Nothing Is Hidden*. Oxford: Blackwell, 1986.

Sartre, Jean-Paul, *The Psychology of Imagination*. Translated by B. Frechtman. New York: Washington Square Press, 1966.

INDEX